The Art of Marketing for Professional Photographers

◆

Gene Ho

iUniverse, Inc.
New York   Bloomington

The Art of Marketing for Professional Photographers

iUniverse books may be ordered through booksellers or by contacting:

iUniverse
1663 Liberty Drive
Bloomington, IN 47403
www.iuniverse.com
1-800-Authors (1-800-288-4677)

Because of the dynamic nature of the Internet, any Web addresses or links contained in this book may have changed since publication and may no longer be valid.

ISBN: 978-1-4502-4009-3 (sc)
ISBN: 978-1-4502-4210-3 (dj)
ISBN: 978-1-4502-4209-7 (ebk)

Printed in the United States of America

iUniverse rev. date: 8/12/2010

To my mother…

And with special thanks:

Nadean Bruehlman
Emily Massingill
Brandon Hedgpeth

Contents

Foreword

By Emily Massingill

I get the question all the time.

As a newspaper editor, people always ask me how long I think newspapers will be around.

I'm never quite sure how to answer, and in all honesty I really don't know.

I can't predict the future.

I like to think some newspapers will reach into another decade or so.

I live and work in places where there are plenty of people who aren't "screen people."

They still handwrite things. They don't know what "that internet" is. They want to turn pages.

But I also know many people who have lost their job in the newspaper world. It's evolving at a rapid pace.

Photographers are experiencing the same thing. Those in the photography world today don't need to touch and hold their photos. They don't need to turn pages and point to them in a book they keep on a shelf for those who stop by.

I hate to admit it. But I often read my news online. So I guess you can count me in as "part of the problem."

The beautiful thing about the newspaper's demise is that they're not going to be shocked when it comes time to lock the doors to the newsroom and the paper is no longer. They've got fair warning as technology unravels before them – and they're preparing themselves for it.

To do this, I believe, they're learning to market themselves. For many news organizations, doing this the right way just might keep them afloat – just in a different way.

Reporters are covering city council and school board meetings as fast as they're happening. Those city council people have a website – and so does the school. You can click on "news" or "minutes" and find out all you missed.

But the smart, strong papers aren't letting you waste your time there. They're luring you to their website now. They want you to know there will be a place for you to find your news even when it's no longer rolled up and thrown on your front porch.

And right now, they're offering that news to you for free.

I canceled my news subscription months ago, simply because I was getting all I needed to know online.

So even though newspapers in their printed form may eventually go away, there will still be a need for "news." They need people to write those online stories.

Not only that – those newspapers have apps for cell phones and other electronic devices that will make our news even more accessible no matter where we are. They're keeping up. They'll be delivered digitally each day – in the wee morning hours.

The papers that have been smart about their marketing will already have a large group of followers for their online base. Those readers won't head to the school's website for the school news or head to the village's site to see what happened at city council. They'll go right where they've been going along.

And they'll start telling people about it.

The options are unlimited for things like breaking news, audio, video, maps and background stories at, literally, our fingertips. If these newspapers market themselves just right, everyone that reads them now, will read them then.

Think about how that relates to the plight of the pro photographers today.

Today's photographers are shooting like crazy. They're taking millions of photos – and it's cheap to develop and print.

When I walk into an event to cover something anymore – it's not obvious I'm the newspaper reporter. Everywhere I look there are big cameras – many are nicer than mine – and aspiring photographers are everywhere.

I can only imagine the challenges they are facing.

So how can these photographers meet the challenges of a changing work dynamic?

It's by staying ahead of the game.

Gene Ho and his photographers are forward thinking.

Just like those newspapers, Gene is finding ways beyond photos to keep his following strong.

And here, Gene shares exactly how he's doing it.

Preface

I am not a professional author.

I'm not even a professional photography instructor.

Sure. I've penned a couple of books.

And yes... I do give talks and workshops.

But when someone asks me? I tell them that I'm a professional photographer.

Ah... love the sound of that.

What I do for a living... I would do it for free.

Shhh...

Don't tell anyone.

I also like to get paid.

But at the same time, it's not the money that motivates me.

I live in a resort town, and someone had this shirt on that said, "A bad day fishing is better than a good day at work."

I beg to differ.

A bad day at work for me is still better than a good day fishing.

But the irony of it all?

The true irony of it?

It's one in the same.

Some people like to fish for flounder?

I like to fish for clients. I like to fish for brides.

And the chase is half the fun.

And that's where marketing comes in.

This book tells you all about how I get my clients. How I market myself. How I grow my studio.

That being said, you might ask, "why?"

Why would I sit here and put down on paper what I do?

For starters, I'm not primarily motivated by money.

I am motivated by a passion for photography.

Secondly… I realize that there are few secrets in the photography world.

What you do today will be copied tomorrow.

Back in the day, it would take months – maybe years before word got out about the next big thing.

But today? What you do gets instantly passed on through internet forums and becomes open viewing.

So how is this book different?

This book is about principles.

It's not telling you step by step how to do things.

If it was a "step by step" – this book would be quickly outdated.

But principles don't get outdated like that.

Because YOU build upon the principles.

You take what I've outlined here and YOU take it to the next level.

It's the same way you learned photography.

Maybe you took a class. Or maybe you learned on your own.

But if your skills are at a professional level?

Chances are?

Chances are that you FEEL your photos.

Sure. Someone can say to you, "Under these circumstances – do this. Put the person's hand here. Have them turn this way."

But in reality... if you're remotely successful, you feel your way through it.

You take what you've learned and make a small adjustment here – a small adjustment there – and you create.

If you can create with photography... then why not with marketing for photography?

So here it is.

My guide on how it's done.

Chapter 1

The Game

The game used to be easier.

The rules - much more simple.

The better the photographer you were? The more work you got.

How things have changed.

When I first started photography 18 years ago... it seemed each city had a "patriarch" of sorts.

One... maybe two photographers that everyone looked up to.

They got all the work - while the ends were thrown out to us start-ups.

And it was a game we were willing to play.

We were shooting with film.

And the advantage went with the photographers who had years of experience behind them.

There was no such thing as looking at the back of your camera to make sure you "got it."

Today… it's possible for a new photographer to get really good - really fast.

It is what it is.

Where back in the days of film? You had to learn… shoot and adjust.

Now? It's shoot and look at the back of your camera - and adjust.

So today?

You have old-timers competing with start ups. Start ups who enter the field dominating right off the bat.

While the old-timers can complain that the new crop of photographers don't really know much about balanced fill-flash or even how to use a light meter.

The fact is that it's possible to get real good - real fast as a photographer.

Don't get me wrong.

I realize that it's still about the photography.

But today you have more and more photographers shooting at an elite level that are barely struggling to get by.

I'm floored when I see this.

Basically, there is a new class of photographers shooting at an amazing skill level - but barely able to make ends meet.

So what makes the difference between one elite photographer that works and one that doesn't?

Marketing.

It's the fact that one photographer is able to get the jobs and the other is not.

It's the ability to draw paying clients to you.

And this is what this book is about.

Back then? The rules were simple.

Everything revolved around one thing - your Yellow Page ad.

And the formula was pretty simple.

You bought an ad in the Yellow Pages.

And the big boys? They were buying full-page Display Ads.

Meanwhile... the start-ups?

I bought my little "in column" ad. And as I made more money - my ad would get bigger.

It was pretty obvious in each city what the pecking order was.

You could tell who the players were and who weren't.

Of course... I would mix it up.

Some of the more crafty photographers would do mall displays and tap into other forms of advertising.

And yes... there was "word of mouth."

But that was the game.

You worked - you put an ad in the Yellow Pages.

Today? Today, the game has changed.

Marketing for professional photographer has now become an art form.

And as with any true art - there is no formula.

There's not just one thing you're "supposed to do."

There's no "script" to follow.

In the world today? There are so many businesses that stick to a script.

Think about how many times you had a problem with "customer service" at some business.

"I understand your frustration, we are sorry. But there is nothing we can do at this point."

You just want to scream, "Hello!!! I am a real human being! Can we cut through the red tape!?!"

But much of the world is made up of businesses that stick to a script.

Here's a great example of doing what you're *supposed* to do in every day life.

OK... I spend a lot of time in my car.

And I try to plan my schedule and eat well when I'm on the road.

But this time? I pull up in to this fast food place.

Normally - I try to avoid places like that. But sometimes choices are limited.

So I walk into this "restaurant" and I can tell things aren't good.

There's a line and the people in front of me are all ticked off.

And by the time I get to the cashier - I figure out why.

It was near closing time. And the place was basically out of chicken.

And it was pretty obvious.

"Um... OK... I can see you are about to close. What do you have left?"

She replies... "Well... what do you want?"

Interesting. Looks like they're out of chicken...

"Can I have a 3 piece dark?"

So no go.

"Sir... No. We're out of that."

OK...

"Fine... um... Can I have a drumstick and some mash potatoes?"

And I knew. And I can't believe I'm going through the motions.

"Sir... we're out of that as well."

At this time... I'm tired of playing her game.

I can tell there's only one piece of chicken left in the whole place.

I can see it. I'm looking at it!

But I guess she has to follow some script.

"I tell you what... I can see that you have one piece of chicken left. Can I just buy that?

Her eyes lit up.

"Sure. One chicken breast."

She enters that into cash register.

Then she asks...

"Original, Crispy or Grilled?"

That is corporate America in a nutshell.

Will we be like that?

Will we do things because that's the way we were told it HAS to be done?

If you want to succeed as a pro photographer? You can find a script and work with it.

You may or may not succeed.

You may or may not succeed because you're following someone else's pattern.

You are following THEIR script that worked for THEM.

With YOUR studio... are YOU following a script?

Are we as wedding photographers doing a bridal show because we were told we have to do a bridal show?

Are we as portrait photographers spending all our time marketing online - because that's what we were told to do?

Even more today - there's really not any kind of formula for success.

Most everything works - but only under certain conditions.

It may or may not work - depending on each person's individual circumstances.

There is no ONE formula.

If that wasn't the case? All we would ALL have to do is hop on Facebook, network a little. And we'd all be booking jobs.

Can it be done that way? Of course!

But does a big back cover ad in a prominent magazine also work?

Yep.

So how do you do it?

How do you carve out a marketing plan that is effective?

For starters, it starts with you.

It starts with your passion as a photographer.

I'm sure that you can succeed financially in photography without passion.

But I strongly suspect that the bottom line is still about the love of photography.

So that's it for starters.

From there? It's just getting your message out.

When I started as a professional photographer 19 years ago as a 22 year-old start up, I had a mad passion for photography.

Loved it. Still do.

But even back then, I knew it was about translating my love for photography to the general public.

And to do that? I used every conceivable angle to get the message out.

The message?

"I'm new. I have new ideas. I'm here."

Nearly 20 years later... I'm still screaming that message from the rooftops.

If there's a proof point. Today? My ideas are still as fresh as ever.

My clients still see me as cutting edge.

They see me as a photographer with fresh ideas.

They see me as someone who loves photography.

And they see me just as hungry as ever.

The truth of the matter is - I love photography.

It's my passion. It's my career. It's my hobby.

But how that message gets out to the general public is by means of marketing.

Over my 20 years as a photographer... I've touched on almost ALL of it.

Almost every imaginable marketing plan has been tried by me.

Almost every imaginable advertising program has been bought by me. Paid for and executed.

My thoughts on it all?

For starters... there's no "right way" to do it.

But that's what makes this discussion so interesting.

There's no "point by point" marketing system you can follow... nor could I teach.

But I can teach you concepts. I can teach you ideas.

And I can teach you lessons based on experience.

Some that work. Some that I tried with... and failed.

Some that worked way back when. Some that work now.

In this book... I will share it all with you. The triumphs and the failures.

A collection of ideas and case studies.

And between it all? Perhaps.

Perhaps you can find a way to position yourself in what has become a tangled web of professional photography today.

How can you stand out amongst the crowded field of very talented new photographers?

Let me please show you.

Chapter 2

Power Marketing Defined

I'm not exactly a business wunder-kind.

I know from a distance it seems pretty nifty with me running a high-profile photography studio.

But I think it starts and stops there.

I've had other businesses before.

And I've failed at them.

Some were mildly successful. Others a disaster.

But the one thing that has lasted is my photography business.

I even hate calling it a business.

I despise that word.

Because it puts it on the level of a cold corporation.

My studio isn't like that.

My photography studio is an outlet for my soul.

But the truth is… as long as I can make money from photography - then the longer I can pursue this career.

So that's where the marketing part comes in.

I don't know how marketing is defined by the business experts.

I'm not an expert at business.

I wouldn't even say I'm an expert at marketing.

But I am an expert in marketing for professional photographers.

And with that... I added the word "Power" in front of it.

Power Marketing for Professional Photographers.

My definition...

Power Marketing: *Minimal Resources for Maximum Returns.*

In the business world... they have term for this.

They call it ROI... or Return on Investment.

OK... This is kind of the same.

Or at least the idea is.

But the reason why I think the ROI logic is faulty when it comes to promoting your photography studio?

Because in the business world? ROI counts actual dollars.

In the photography world... it's not always about actual dollars spent.

See... it's easy to say... "Geez... just generated all these shoots... and I didn't even spend a dime."

Trust me... that is REALLY good.

But it doesn't mean that you spend zero dollars.

OK... you probably did spend "zero" dollars... but you ate up all your resources - your time... in generating those shoots.

What the focus on Power Marketing is - is "Minimal Resources for Maximum Returns."

OK... I'm not making a case for or against "low budget" marketing. For example... marketing on Facebook or Twitter...

And I'm certainly not making a case for or against "big budget" marketing. For example... ads in magazines or billboards.

But rather - what resources you are putting out PER campaign...

Those resources could be actual dollars. It could be the time you put in.

And... if you spend dollars... how can you maximize those dollars?

If you spend time? How do you maximize that time?

That is really the key to it all.

In other words... it's not what you do. It's how you do it.

I always think back to those old Kung Fu movies.

"Master... they are talking trash to us! We must avenge our brother!"

Basically... we can debate all day long.

It's not a matter of "My Kung Fu Master is greater than your Kung Fu Master."

If I said - "magazine ads" were the way to go.

They you can do all your research and find out data on how that's NOT the way to go.

There's just no one way.

Rather - it's being smart about it and developing an effective marketing campaign.

And that's the hard part.

The hard part is figuring out what works for you.

The key to marketing powerfully?

Start by understanding what you're trying to market in the first place.

Chapter 3

Identify What You Are Selling

That's simple right?

I'm selling photos.

Or... I'm selling wedding photos. Or portraits.

That is where the mistake starts.

To illustrate?

Lets take 100 photographers.

Put them all in one city.

And give each one - one category in the Yellow Pages.

So in "Photographers - Portraits" - you would have maybe 40 names.

In "Photographers - Weddings" - you would maybe 30 names. And then the same for say the Commercial category.

So what have we come up with?

Basically just a list of photographers and what they do.

It's what NOT to do in a nutshell.

And here's why.

No one cares.

They get it. You're a photographer.

You photograph stuff.

There are tons of us around.

What you have to do is figure out what you're REALLY selling and market THAT.

What are you really selling?

Currently? My studio is selling "Cutting Edge and Class."

That wasn't always the case.

When I first started photography? I was selling "Friendly Service and Dependability."

Was I cutting edge 19 years ago? Sure.

Do I offer friendly service now? Of course.

But I pick what I'm trying to sell - so I know what I'm doing.

I know what I'm trying to market in the first place.

To do this? I start by telling MYSELF what I'm saying in REAL WORLD terms.

OK... ready for me to get brutally honest?

Forget the cute tag lines.

What I'm marketing right now is "Cutting Edge and Class."

But what that REALLY means?

"Hey... with my studio? You're going to get some really good stuff. I'm going to push the envelope and I'm going to find angles in my pictures that you never dreamed of. But at the same time? Trust me... we're no start-up studio. Our clients are big time and high end."

So that's my message.

And that's what I'm currently selling.

When I first started photography? My cute little tag line was "Friendly Service and Dependable."

But when I was a 22-year-old pro photographer? That's what I was selling.

What that REALLY means?

"Hey… dude. You're going to want to go with me. Because if you go with the other photographers here - they are jerks. I'm not a jerk, because I'm new at this. And I'm hungry for work and I'm happy to be here. But at the same time… don't think I'm some kid that won't show up to your wedding. I'm dependable."

See?

A lot of photographers don't succeed in effectively marketing their studio, because they don't even know what they are marketing in the FIRST place.

You have to start by figuring this out.

Who are you?

What makes you different?

Here's another one.

And here is me bearing my soul.

It's really hard to do anything for 18 years and not go through some rough patches.

At one time in my career (maybe about 10 years ago…)

But at one time I developed the reputation of being "good - but slow."

Basically… my studio was already established.

Our work was excellent and my studio already had a reputation for turning out some really fine photography.

But I tell you? We couldn't get our product out in time.

The problem was partly due to distractions in my personal life.

The other problem was there was just too much turn-around at my studio.

My staff photographers were leaving and starting their own studios.

I would hire new photographers - but even then… it takes some time.

And… quite frankly… I was mismanaging the studio funds.

I got into some debt. And it just wasn't easy.

The product I was selling - the pictures themselves. They were second to none.

But the problem was, it took too long to get weddings out. It took forever to get prints out. Albums out.

Everything.

I went through a time when we were REAL slow.

And people know it.

At that time?

It would have be a grand waste of money to start marketing the message "Cutting Edge and Class."

We were already cutting edge. Our clients were already classy.

If I would have continued with that marketing buzz word?

I would have been sunk.

Everyone would have said… "Yeah… Cutting Edge - if you can even get your wedding album before your first child is born."

So for a two-year period… I picked a different cutesy tagline.

My new tagline was, "Dependability."

At the time? I didn't need to prove myself as cutting edge.

I didn't need to prove myself as "Friendly."

We were ALREADY friendly.

How can we NOT be friendly?

I'm sitting there trying to explain to my clients why they won't have their wedding pictures for another three weeks.

I was plenty friendly.

But what I needed to do is market myself as dependable.

That was my tagline.

But what I was REALLY selling.

"Hey... You know. I really do understand that I'm slow. I realize people are saying that it takes forever for them to get their stuff from me. But I tell you what. We ARE dependable."

So I started this new marketing campaign.

And that probably saved my studio from absolute ruin.

Basically I marketed a guarantee for my wedding photography.

In short... if we were one week late? The bride would get $200 worth of reprints for free.

If we were two weeks late? The bride would get $400 worth of reprints - all for free.

If we were three weeks late? We would refund the whole package.

I wrote that guarantee onto my rate cards and marketed that message.

Granted - I still had to deliver the product.

I think during that whole time I gave way probably 3 or 4 reprint credits.

And in one case, I gave a full refund back to the bride and groom.

But that was my message.

And it was one that I need to share with everyone.

Think about you.

What message do you want to get out?

Let's say that you are a part-time professional photographer.

You know you're good. But you're good where you're at in life.

There's no way in the world you would ever want to be a Gene Ho and deal with all the volume.

You do want more work - but you have a lot of obligations. Maybe another job that has great benefits.

Or… maybe you have a family.

Trust me. A marketing campaign with a "Friendly and Dependable" tagline probably won't work for you.

People already know you're dependable.

You're a Mom.

Plus… you want to work more - but just with the high-end clients.

Thus… "Personalized One on One Service" might be what you are REALLY selling.

In real world terms?

"Hey… I'm a great photographer. But you won't find me with a big studio downtown because I don't care for that. But if you hire me? I'll shoot great photos for you, but I also won't be too busy to sit down and have a cup of coffee with you."

See how this works?

Before you can even begin to market yourself - you have to figure out what you want to market in the FIRST place.

If that's you?

What good does it do to run an ad saying that you do shoot weddings?

If you're selling weddings? You got plenty of competition.

One of them being ME.

But if you were a little more clever?

Then you're NOT selling weddings.

Your selling Personalized Service. Personalized service that you may or may not get with some big old - corporate studio.

No… you're selling personal service. One-on-one service where you'll remember your clients name and how many squirts of Hazelnut syrup goes with their Latte.

So do some thinking.

Find out what you are selling.

Find out how you are different from the other photographers working your area.

Once you know that? You can figure where to start in crafting your marketing strategy.

Chapter 4

What the Font?

I found that most photographers are clueless about fonts.

They've spent all their time crafting their photography - but they have little or no understanding of the use of fonts.

Words have power.

The way words look, have even more power.

They convey messages.

Take time to understand and learn fonts.

From there… you can properly match your message with your fonts.

Here's the object lesson.

And we're taking this to an extreme.

You are familiar with what an Old English font looks like, correct?

Sometimes it's called the Shakespeare font.

You know how it looks. It's really "foo foo" - is the best I can describe it.

In short - businesses like "Medieval Times" - the dinner show... they use that font in their ads.

That's perfect.

It has the feel of something old.

OK... now this is an extreme.

But if the message of your studio was Modern and Chic... would you use and Old English font?

No way.

But my point is... you can see how that doesn't match.

Another font - Comic Sans.

It's a cutesy font that sends a message of fun times.

It's loose... it's fun. And a lot of the comic strips use it as their font of choice.

Now... would you use that font if your studio's marketing messages was, "Responsible and Safe?"

No.

And off hand - that's not a bad marketing message to have.

Maybe your area has had a bunch of start-up photographers that failed.

Maybe you FEEL that the community is starting to get scared of new photographers.

Sometimes that happens when you hear news reports of some bride that never got her wedding pictures.

The news reporter flashes up this picture of a studio and says, "It's been three months... and Janie still didn't get her pictures."

OK... so the whole community is a panic.

But say you have been in business a long time.

Your studio is established.

A brief marketing campaign might be in order. Responsible. Safe. Established.

Nice! Sign me up.

Your work might be crap, but at least I'm going to get my pictures.

Just kidding.

But if I was having an ad campaign like this… do you think I would use a Comic Sans font?

No way.

Think about when I was trying to regain the community's trust.

I'm trying to tell everyone that you can STILL go with me. That even though I've been slow in the past… that I'm responsible.

Would I make that guarantee with a Comic Sans font?

Granted… that's the extreme.

At that point? It might not be bad to have an Old English font.

Maybe not for the whole thing. But maybe just in the title.

My Guarantee - in bold letters. In an Old English font.

Effective.

I'm here. I'm not going anywhere. I'm like a rock.

However… would I ever use the opposite extreme?

Of course.

Let us say that I've become the establishment.

People have used my studio for years.

But suddenly I've gained the reputation of the safe photographer.

There's no question about it.

I'm here and I'm not going anywhere.

At the same time… let us say that there are new photographers out there.

They are young. They are hip.

I don't need to convince anyone that I'm safe.

So maybe I'll start a marketing campaign to show that I'm fun.

I might use Comic Sans.

Those new photographers? I would suspect it would be a mistake if they every used Comic Sans in their promo material.

We get it. You're obviously young. You're obviously hip.

But give us some assurance.

Not Old English assurance. But something more mature.

Consider that when you are developing your marketing material.

That is… when you are working on your business cards. Your logo. Your website. Your rate card. Your magazine ad.

Consider your fonts.

Old English and Comic Sans are two on the opposite extremes.

But each font tells a story.

Chose carefully.

You want to figure out how I learned what fonts were what?

Here's an interesting exercise that I do.

It starts with picking up a local magazine.

Any magazine.

Just make sure it's local. It could even be a vacation guide.

You don't want to play this game with national magazines.

Because usually - with big budget national magazines - they have professional ad designers that know all this stuff.

But with local magazines - it's filled with people that REALLY know what they are doing and people that REALLY have no clue.

When I travel... I always try to pick up one of the magazines.

This is what I do.

I take a pen... and I circle each ad and write in what I think about each ad.

And these aren't photographers.

These are local businesses.

Some of my thoughts?

"High-end."

"Cheap."

"Responsible."

"Hide your Children."

Now that's not to say that "Cheap" is bad.

For photographers - that might be a bad thing.

But maybe it's a plumber.

When I hire a plumber... I just want to make sure that I can flush a toilet and not have to jiggle the handle.

I don't care if I have to look at your butt crack.

I just want you to fix my toilet and I don't want to pay a lot of money for it.

So to be honest, if I saw an ad for a plumber and I needed a plumber?

I'd probably pick the one that looked like they were cheap.

So if you study that ad? Ask yourself what makes it so that plumber looks inexpensive?

What fonts did the company use?

Lets say it's a restaurant.

Circle an ad and write in what thought comes to mind when you see that ad.

If I want to take out some clients to a nice dinner, I might want something high-end.

Do you see something high end?

And if so… what is it about the ad? What is it about the font… that shows it's high end?

Or…

Or is it clearly a high-end restaurant - but they totally fail and the ad makes it look like they are cheap.

There is a restaurant called "Dick's Last Resort."

The ad designer is brilliant.

They use a font very similar to Comic Sans.

But I look at that ad and it screams out fun. And this is based on the font alone.

But they are going for that.

They have a message - and they hit that message on the head - based upon words and the way the words look.

So study these ads and learn from them.

See what the company is trying to portray itself as.

And see if they accomplish this.

Fonts are your first foot forward.

Most of us don't have pictures as our logo.

Am I correct?

We have WORDS as our logos.

Those words... the way it looks, conveys EVERYTHING about our studio.

The company, "Toys R Us."

Brilliant logo. A fun logo.

They even have the R backwards on it.

Hey... fun, fun, fun!

But it's about the font.

Now take a look at your promotional material.

Take a look at your logo.

Everything counts.

Even the size of your font counts.

As a general rule - the smaller-sized fonts (8 points and 10 points) - give an impression of intelligence.

As the fonts get bigger - it leans toward being more simple.

But the point is? Sometimes you WANT that.

Sometimes you WANT to create an ad that denotes your simplicity.

If you want to master the art of marketing - as a photographer anyway...

Study the fonts.

Study how they look and what thoughts they convey.

And this is important - because if you're like me? Your marketing needs are ever changing.

Sometimes your studio needs to be portrayed as fun.

Sometimes your studio needs to be portrayed as serious.

Use your fonts to carry these thoughts out.

Chapter 5

Your Promo Pictures

Most photographers to a pretty good job selecting the pictures they use for promotion.

At the same time, here are a few thoughts to consider.

For starters - I have a general rule on pictures I chose for display.

It's a simple rule: **You get what you're fishing with.**

For example... if you want high-end weddings in exotic locations? You need to show high-end weddings in exotic locations.

If you want high-end family portraits, then you need to show high-end family portraits.

Quite frankly, maybe you don't want that. I mean, sure it would be nice.

But in some resort areas - families don't want a big to-do.

What they are looking for is some great family photos on the beach.

Not that they are any less "high-end" - but they are on vacation and they don't want to dress their children up in white Victorian-era outfits.

They are looking for a casual beach portrait.

If you want that type of work… are you SHOWING that type of work?

This seems so amazingly basic.

But it is shocking how many times this not being done.

I see photographers who want one type of customer - but they are fishing with a completely different set of "bait."

I've done it before.

For years - my studio has had a huge presence in the coastal resort areas of the south.

When we first started to break into other markets - we found we would get the destination brides - but not weddings held at the actual cities.

Why was that?

For starters: Our portfolios were filled with pictures of brides getting married on the beach.

That's neat.

And all those brides living in cities like Atlanta and Charlotte?

They would hire us.

But most of our clients there were already getting married on the coast.

They were having a destination wedding in Charleston, South Carolina and just "happened" to run into us at a bridal show in Charlotte.

Sure. We would get a fair share of weddings in these other inland cities.

But we were able to turn it into overdrive by making one small adjustment.

We started displaying weddings with local landmarks that each city had a presence in.

In other words… we had Atlanta promo material. We had Charlotte promo material. Same for Reno. And the same for everywhere else.

We were using the correct bait - for each specific area.

We wanted more Atlanta brides? We needed to use Atlanta bride "bait."

Match your portfolio to the types of clients you want.

Match your marketing material to the clients you want.

That being said --

Take it one step further.

Make sure your pictures match your message.

Again. I'll use the most extreme case possible.

Not that you would do this… but just to make a point.

If your message is "Playful and Fun" - make sure your photos look playful and fun.

And remember…

Your marketing strategy is the OVERALL theme.

Like all your ads don't have to say: "We're FUN! Look at us!"

But your clients are smart.

And as long as your pictures and message match what you're trying to do, the public will get it.

Make your pictures match your message.

Case in point.

OK… me, personally?

At my wedding… I wanted it fun. But at the same time, I wanted it with a certain decorum.

I'm not knocking how other people do it.

But I did not want my the DJ calling my mom out to the dance floor to put on a construction guy hat and do the YMCA.

I think it's fun. It's neat.

I've seen a hundred different ways you can incorporate a rubber chicken into the cake cutting.

It's the same for the wedding DJs.

You get what you're fishing for.

If I'm shopping for a DJ… I'm not going to go with one that features guests doing the Chicken Dance.

But I might go with the one that might feature a picture of an elegant bride and groom dancing.

To me, that would translate more to what I'm looking for.

I guess if there's a mistake to be made?

It would be not knowing what you're marketing for in the first place.

I've seen that before too.

The other danger is trying to market to ALL aspects of the spectrum.

Some photographers try to be a "Jack of all Trades."

So they have a little bit of everything.

That might be good in your portfolio.

But it might spell disaster for a marketing campaign.

Pick a message - and match your photos to that message.

In regards to photos in promo material is picking a picture that has limited appeal.

OK… a secret.

Not always.

But a lot of my marketing pictures involve a silhouette.

That's because I want my brides to imagine THEMSELVES in my pictures.

A silhouette is dreamy.

It's anonymous.

I don't use it all the time. But when I do? It's effective.

It's a picture that has mass appeal.

That being said... I've seen so many pictures that have next to zero mass appeal.

Case in point.

And again. I'm using the MOST extreme case possible.

At the same time, I've seen this done before by more than one photographer.

The photographer takes a picture of a bride - in her dress visiting the graveyard.

OK... I more than get it.

It tells a powerful story.

And the bride probably went on and on about how that picture was amazing.

Most likely someone close to her died just before the wedding and she was taking time out of her special day to honor that person.

If any of us were put in that position, I'm sure we would take the most amazing photos.

But that photo has limited appeal.

There's an interesting story to go along with that.

And just as a side note.

I was overseeing the production of one of my studio's 30-second TV commercials.

So I picked a theme: Elegant and Cutting Edge.

I made the pictures on my commercial match.

So I gave it to one of my photographers who also works video for a sister company of my studio.

The commercial was a slideshow where I wanted classical music to go with my photos.

The night before - I sampled tons of songs.

I finally settled on one of them.

Now, I can't even remember what the song was.

But I thought at the time it was perfect.

So I gave the pictures - my concept and the song - to Heather Moore, the studio's video expert.

The next day… she came back with the product.

"So you know… I made two versions," she said.

So she plays the first one.

Wow. GREAT!

Seemed perfect.

The pictures all "changed over" on cue. Like, the music and the slide show seemed to "dance" together.

"I love it!" I said.

So then Heather tells me to hold on while she shows me the other commercial.

"OK… I made an alternate version with this other song. Because the song you picked was is C minor."

Heather is one of the studio's lead photographers. But she grew up studying music and plays the violin.

"Yeah… most songs in a minor key are not happy songs," she said.

She then played the second version of the commercial to a different song. And it was incredible.

It made all the difference in the world.

The first song sounded more like a song that you would hear in a funeral.

The second song - was upbeat.

The lesson? Match your message.

Chapter 6

Think Like Your Client

I'm sure if you research it, you'll find tons of marketing campaigns that have failed and some that were successful.

But I'll start with two examples of my own.

The first is where I didn't think like the client.

The second is when I did.

Not that all of my mistakes are "way back when."

But this one does fall into the "way back when" category.

And I'm NOT saying that a strategy like this wouldn't work.

I'm just saying that it was the wrong strategy for me at the time.

The idea was brilliant - it was just poorly executed.

I was trying to create some kind of loyalty program.

My "merchant vendor" at the time had gift cards.

In other words, the company that processes my Visa and Mastercard purchases... they had these gift cards.

The way it worked: You buy these gift cards that look and feel like a credit card.

But the cool thing is that you could customize how these cards look.

My plan was that I would get these gift cards. I could sell some as gift cards. I can give some as VIP cards with money set into it.

To be honest? I thought this would be the next big thing.

I envisioned all these people that would have my gift card in their wallets. All with a reminder of my studio every time they sorted through their credit cards.

Deep down inside, I was sure this could work.

I still feel it's a concept that is two screws away from being operational.

But here were my mistakes.

For starters - I didn't think like my clients.

Here's why:

1) I chose the wrong picture to go on my gift cards.

At the time, I had just taken some pictures of a beautiful model.

I thought, "Hey... she would be perfect for this card. I got this sexy girl on my gift card.

Not to say sex doesn't sell.

But it doesn't sell when your clients are mostly families and brides.

For starters, I didn't even identify WHO I was trying to sell to.

And, I also didn't think like my client.

Think about it this way.

Let's say I promote this gift card to my brides.

I tell them, "…and if your parents want to help you buy some wedding prints - they can just buy one of these gift cards. If they buy $200 worth of prints - I'll throw in an extra $50 on me."

And so what?

They buy a gift card from me. I "charge it up" with $250. And I collect $200 from it.

And then what?

The mother of the groom gives her soon-to-be daughter-in-law a gift card with some hot babe on it?

Or think about this…

Some guy comes into my studio.

He wants to buy his wife a Mother's Day present.

Of course, Gene Ho is just an amazing photographer.

So he thinks that it would be a great idea that he buys his wife a gift card from Gene Ho.

OK… all good.

So he comes to my studio, and what?

He's going to buy a gift card with some other woman on it?

"Here you go honey! Happy Mother's Day! Nice card, huh? That girl is HOT!"

2) I didn't think about how people REALLY are.

You know… I am ALSO a consumer.

I buy gift cards all the time.

In fact, gift cards are the currency of choice for MY clients.

I can't tell you the amount of times that one of the Gene Ho Photography brides will come to me and say, "Hey… we just want to thank your photographer for doing such a great job at our wedding. We didn't get a chance to tip him on wedding night. Could we get him a gift card?"

See… THAT is how real people think.

And that's why I love the concept of gift cards.

I use gift cards all the time.

But mostly I use them for SMALL purchases.

For the MOST part - people use gift cards as a de facto way of thanking someone.

If I wanted to thank my lawn guy, and I knew he was a big coffee drinker?

What do you think would be better?

Take $10 out of my pocket and slip it to him… "Here ya go buddy. Good job. Way to keep those weeds out of the yard. Man, I hate it when those weeds come out of the crack of the driveway. Yeah. You're the man. Here's 10 bucks."

Really. How offensive is that?

But I love gift cards, because if I want to thank someone - I can say, "Hey man. Thanks. I know you also love coffee like me. So I got your next cup."

So I give him a Starbucks card for $10.

Or maybe if I'm feeling more generous… I can say I got your next lunch.

And I hand him a $25 gift card to his favorite restaurant.

That's how real people think.

But real people hire a professional photographer, when?

Maybe twice a year?

In some cases - twice in a lifetime. Really, think about it.

I drink coffee everyday.

And I eat lunch everyday.

I'm not saying it doesn't work.

But most people won't keep my gift card handy.

As if, "Ya never know when you're riding down the street and you want to get a headshot - ya know?!"

No. It's not how it works in real life.

THINK like your client.

People do buy me Starbucks gift cards as a thank you.

And I appreciate that.

And I almost always keep one with me.

Because very well, I might be driving down the road and that green Starbucks logo beckons me. And I pull over and buy a cup of coffee with my gift card.

Even if someone WOULD buy my gift card - it's unlikely they would keep it in their wallet as a reminder.

So you can see why this gift card promo was a disaster for me.

I also made another mistake.

This was totally unrelated to marketing.

But I "minted" a ton of these cards.

Basically, I "activated" a bunch of them.

So I had my piles of $100 gift cards. $200 gift cards. $400 gift cards.

But at the time, I didn't realize that my Visa Merchant deducted money from each one after a while.

Like if you power up a $100 gift card - six months later, the gift card would be worth $99.50 as a service charge.

Basically, it was a disaster from beginning to end.

As a footnote: My studio now uses Gift Certificates.

We like them better, because we print them out ourselves. We put the exact dollar amount on them. And we put an expiration date on them.

But yes. I messed up big time on the gift cards.

OK… so that was me NOT thinking like my clients.

Here's an example of me thinking LIKE my clients.

Prestige is a big thing in wedding photography.

I realize this.

But in my particular case - I had a unique problem.

People wanted to book ME.

If you know anything about my business model… I structure my studio by booking multiple photographers every weekend.

My studio currently has 18 photographers - and on any given weekend - I send them out all over the country to do weddings.

The problem I was having was that the brides wanted to book me PERSONALLY.

Normally, this is a good problem to have.

But with my business model - that is NOT a good thing.

So I had a plan.

For starters, I have never set myself above my staff photographers.

I've never said, "Hey… my photographers are really good. But if you want ME, then you need to pay $2,000 more."

Does that business model work?

Of course it does.

There are many photographers out there that have associate photographers.

Yes. If I'm personally booked - you can still have my associate photographer for THIS price.

Again... I'm not saying that way doesn't work.

But my strategy is indeed telling my clients - if you book Gene Ho Photography... you're going to get World Class Photography.

If you book ME personally? You're going to get World Class Photography.

But if you book one of my wedding photographers? You will still get World Class Photography.

Since I started this... there have never been two prices.

There was never one price for me, and one price for my photographers.

To me? Doing that would send mixed messages.

Basically, I would be saying, "Hey! My photographers are JUST as good as me. But by the way... if you want Gene Ho himself? Yeah. Um... I cost $2,000 more."

For starters, I don't believe my Lead Photographers are better than me.

I believe they are equal to me.

And to be brutally honest, my photographers are incredible. On any given day - I might be better than them. Or they might be better than me.

So that being said --

I came up with a marketing campaign.

The gist of it?

"…I might not even be the best photographer on my staff."

Basically, I was telling everyone - "Hey… I know I can shoot a pretty good wedding. But if you think I'm all that? Well think again. Because some of my "employees" are better than me."

Was this a lie?

No way.

Anyone who knows anything about my studio knows how good the Gene Ho Photographers are.

And to prove it, in the upcoming next year - I'm not even the most booked in my studio.

Some of my photographers have already outbooked me.

And that's a good thing.

But I've always loved this campaign…

That is the "I might not even be the best photographer on my staff" campaign.

And it was wildly successful.

I didn't make my staff of photographers anonymous.

I used them in all of my advertisements.

I put their name in magazine ads and in television commercials.

The message?

"Yeah. I'm good. But check out these guys…"

Not only was it the truth.

But I was thinking like my clients.

Really.

For some brides, it's a matter of pride.

They want the best of everything.

They want the best dress. The best cake. The best photographer.

But the point being:

I market my studio so my clients know they are getting the best even if Gene Ho himself is not booked.

Again… it's how I roll.

Will I one day say, "Hey… if you want to book my company, cool. But if you want me, you need to pay $1,000 more."

I doubt it.

I really do.

Actually, maybe yes.

One day, when I'm old and fragile.

I want to do just *one more* wedding.

I want to be so famous that everyone knows my name. But I want to be old enough that I have a walker with cut out tennis balls on the feet.

Sure. I want to come out from the midst of retirement with an oxygen tank.

And some tube on my nose.

Then I will say, "If you want Gene Ho… pay me $3,000 more."

Until then, it's cool.

I'll charge the same as what my other photographers make.

And I want my clients to know that as well.

My studio is about high-end photography.

And I may or may not be personally available.

But thinking like my client?

It's all cool.

Because they know they're getting the best - whether it's me or one of my photographers.

And that's the truth.

Chapter 7

Don't Get High on Your Own Supply

The quote came from the movie "Scarface."

In the movie they called it, "Rule Number Two."

It was in reference to Scarface not getting high on the same drugs he sold.

Of course, I'm not talking about drugs here.

But I am talking about something that can sink you just as badly.

I know, because I've been there.

Even today… my studio's advertising budget is quite strong.

I probably spend more money on advertising in a year than most photography studios gross.

But let me tell you about how it's different from what I used to do.

There was a time I overspent in advertising.

The dollar amount was staggering.

It was as if I was addicted to promotion.

Back page magazine ads. Television commercials. Movie theatre promotions.

All of which were financed by me.

Which is all good and fine.

If all the advertisements were working.

Not all ads work effectively.

So what happened is ad dollars I was spending were choking the life out of my studio.

Some worked great. Others didn't.

I knew it was time to change something.

To be honest? It's very hard to spend zero dollars on advertising.

I'm sure it can be done... but it's not easy.

Even some marketing campaigns - which can be disguised as having no money involved - can actually involve a lot of money and or time.

But whenever possible... don't use your own money to advertise.

Don't get High on Your Own Supply.

Here's how I learned this.

About five years ago, I decided to put a cap on all my ad spending.

I knew I couldn't do it totally.

But I did cap it to the once proven method that worked for my studio in the past.

We have always been very successful at working bridal shows.

So for a one-year period, I told myself I would only spend real money on the shows.

Everything had to sink or swim on its own.

The result was that I learned to be incredibly crafty in creating advertising campaigns without spending my own money.

As you could imagine... most of these have to do with trades.

People still need photos. And we still need advertising.

We've traded out with televisions stations – headshots for commercial time.

We've traded out with radio stations – event photography for radio commercial time.

We've traded out with the local symphony. Headshots of the conductor and their musicians for an ad in their playbill. Not to mention, two season tickets.

The trade offs are literally pennies on the dollar.

And to them? The trade off for THEM is literally pennies on the dollar.

Next time you listen to the radio or watch television... try to spot what is called the "house ads."

Quite simply... not all ads get sold.

And the spots that don't get sold - get designated for "house ads."

A house ad might be a commercial that promotes one of the station's agendas.

It could be an event the station is promoting.

It could be a commercial advertising one of the station's sister companies.

Either way... these spots are actually fillers.

And if the radio station, televisions station or even magazine can fill it with something they actually need?

It's a win for them.

My trade policy is what I call, "Retail for Retail" or "Dollar for Dollar."

In other words…

I tell you how much I would charge for the shoot. And you, in turn, give me that same dollar amount in ad money.

We ALL know how this works.

My last trade was headshots at a television station.

A very fair market price for my work came to $2,500.

I didn't rip them off. I didn't over-exaggerate my costs.

I basically took the price of what it would take to do the job. And I gave them that amount.

But we ALL know this.

In REAL WORLD economics.

You know what would happen in REAL life?

They would have said… "Hmmm… $2,500 for a day's shoot. This guy is good. But can we shop around for a few more photographers?"

And for me? In REAL WORLD terms?

Before I buy $2,500 worth of television spots.

I have to ask myself… "Can this money be used in another way?"

In other words… would $2,500 be better spent in another advertising venue?

The truth is? Neither one of us had to debate this.

It's well worth it to me. It was well worth it to them.

That's not to say you should NEVER pay for advertising.

It's just that whenever the opportunity arises, it's a great idea to trade out.

I call this your **Gross Marketing Impact**.

This is the grand number of BOTH your paid advertising and "unpaid" adverting. Plus, it includes the actual value of all your marketing ventures, including trades and partnerships.

Currently my Gross Marketing Impact is about $200,000 a year.

Out of that? Maybe a quarter of it is actual dollars I've spent on real advertising.

The rest of it is advertising based on trades and or joint marketing concepts.

A **Joint Marketing Concept** is when we have partnered up with another business.

Here is an example.

A local gym wanted new photos.

This gym is pretty big and has three locations here.

And a business that size has a pretty formidable advertising budget.

They could easily pay for photos.

I could have easily charged them $1,500 for two shoots over two afternoons.

But always ask yourself if there is a bigger opportunity available.

Rather than just take the $1,500 or so…

I sat down and talked to principal players involved.

This involved more than a trade.

But we decided to work together.

We would get them their photos.

And we also got free gym memberships for my photographers.

Quite frankly, I haven't been there yet. I feel like I get my work out in running around shooting pictures.

But we got something even better than those memberships.

The gym ties us into their advertising.

They promote my studio side by side with them in THEIR ads.

For starters… this is more than just my photos with a tagline, "Gene Ho Photography" on it.

Strive for partnerships.

Work to have your partner businesses promote you side by side.

In this case, the gym shows off our work in their ads. And they prominently credit our photos.

They also promote us to their members.

In return? Besides having a pro photographer at their disposal? We also take care of their members with special deals.

And we actively promote them as well.

I take this advertising campaign and I assign a number to it. That is what it would cost me to buy this advertising if I had paid actual dollars for it.

Try to constantly look for ways to increase your Gross Marketing Impact.

To help yourself?

Keep score.

This is how you start.

Take a piece of paper and look at your year.

Make three columns. "Paid, Unpaid, Total."

In the paid column? Easy.

This year I'm sure you will spend real dollars on advertisements.

So put down in the paid column - "Bridal Show 1 - $700" or "Google Ad Words - $500."

Whatever.

Just write down all your paid ads.

Afterwards? Let's see if you can expand your impact.

On the unpaid side?

Figure out ways to get that number up.

Here's a quick suggestion.

Each year, my studio picks a number out of our collective ass.

It's just a number we happen to feel comfortable with.

This year? We picked $5,000.

So we made $5,000 worth of gift certificates in $300 and $500 denominations.

From there, we wait for the charities to call.

And as long as we deem the charity worthy? We will give those gift certificates out to them.

The math is pretty set in stone.

Most of these charities auction the gift certificates off at their fundraisers.

Normally, a $500 gift certificate will sell at a charity auction for about $300.

It's funny, because sometimes our gift certificates will sell higher than the face amount because someone is trying to "out do" another person.

But this is perfect for us.

The charity gets actual money.

We get to feel great about ourselves because we're helping the community.

But we also get tons of word of mouth.

Granted - we still have to pay.

People do come back and cash in their gift certificates.

But it's well worth it.

$5,000 might be above your tolerance level.

But pick a number.

Any number.

And start "minting" your gift certificates.

If organizations aren't knocking down your door to ask for a donation, knock down their door.

Granted… those gift certificates are about helping the community.

But the community will in turn help you.

But from a strictly economic standpoint?

Work to get your Gross Marketing Impact as high as possible.

You can do it the hard way, by actually paying for it in real world dollars --

Or you can work by spending other people's money.

Either way… you have to pay.

But having a $200,000 marketing impact would not be a possibility for me right now if I had to spend real money on it.

Start small.

Maybe the only thing in your "paid" column is your business cards.

Fine. That's a great place to start.

But then work to build up that number by being creative.

Think of new ways to make the OTHER side go up.

And speaking of business cards…

Chapter 8

Which Came First? The Chicken or The Egg? Or The Business Card

So that's the age-old debate.

Which came first? The chicken or the egg?

Makes me laugh.

You can say the same thing about businesses.

Which came first? The Business or the Business Card.

It seems that even before some businesses are officially licensed… before they are actually IN business?

The owner first has a business card made.

Long, long time ago.

I had a start-up photographer come up to me.

He handed me his business card.

"I just paid $25 for 1,000 of these. If I could just get one job from it, I'll make my money back."

And that's where the mistake begins.

No one gives a crap about a business card.

You can make 20,000 of them and it won't guarantee your going to get a $25 job from it.

If you don't believe me?

Place them. Or rather... account for them.

In the past year... take all the business cards that people have given you. And you tell me which ones you used for a tooth pick and which ones you've saved.

Business cards are so commonplace they've become virtually ineffective.

OK... I get it.

Everyone has a story of how they placed a business card and got some huge account.

So I'm not saying that business cards are worthless.

I'm just saying they have been totally used wrong in real-world marketing.

Next time you're at the grocery store. Next time you're at the coffee house.

See the mass collection of business cards on their community bulletin board.

Do you think that even 10 percent of those business cards have generated one new client?

Again... Not to say I'm anti-business cards.

But perhaps less is more.

Funny story about the one time I wanted to have a business card around.

Last summer I got married.

Pretty neat event. Interesting to be on the other side of the camera like that.

If you're wondering... I got married on a Wednesday.

Because my studio primarily does weddings - I just couldn't stomach the thought of closing off the studio on a Saturday.

So I held my wedding on a Wednesday night.

Anyway... so I held my wedding at one of the Resorts here in Myrtle Beach.

I'm walking into my wedding venue. And if you can believe it... a couple stopped me and asked me to take a picture of them with their camera.

The ONE TIME that I'm going to a wedding and I'm not carrying a camera.

Like they didn't know who I was.

Just some random couple with their camera.

Like they looked at me and said, "There's a Chinese guy. He must be good with a camera."

At first I thought I was getting punked.

Seriously.

I thought my guys were filming me.

But no. Like... I was really being asked to take a picture of a couple on my wedding day.

So they hand me their camera.

And then they give me this 2-minute tutorial on how this camera works.

So I thought I would have some fun.

I pretended not to know how to use it.

"Um... OK... so I press this button?"

And so this guy was trying to tell me how to shoot.

As you can tell... I was really trying to make the best of this.

So finally... I say... "OK... I got it."

And as you can imagine.

He had the camera all in dummy mode.

I'm sorry... I can't shoot a camera when the setting is on Program of any sort.

I think he had it on that "Mountain Setting" or maybe that "Flower Setting."

As if people look and say, "Oh... I'm shooting a flower. Oh look! There's a setting that looks like a flower."

I couldn't do it.

So I messed with all his settings and shot the photo in manual mode.

I tell you... I wish I would have had a business card on me and handed it to him to send me a copy.

But since I don't bring business cards to my own wedding - I didn't have one handy.

So yes. Business cards are important to have.

But use them effectively.

With business cards? I take a less-is-more approach.

Here's how it works.

At least for wedding photographers here...

Have you ever shot a bridal portrait or an engagement shoot that was so incredible - it would knock the socks off of anyone who saw it?

And for all of your good luck... the bride displays this at her wedding.

Granted - that doesn't happen all the time.

Don't you hate it when you do a great shoot - and the bride picks one of the mediocre shots to display?

Oh... burns me.

OK... but here you are. You are at a wedding and your picture on display - is the talk of the reception.

Now at this point... most photographers would be inclined to take a stack of business cards and stick it by the portrait.

I'm not saying this doesn't work.

All I'm saying is consider the benefits of NOT doing this.

How can you benefit by NOT handing out your business cards?

Well consider this.

You have this knock-out picture.

People see it and they say, "Wow... GREAT picture! And... Oh... I see. Gene Ho took that picture."

They see my business card there.

And maybe they even pick one up.

End of the relationship.

Now here's the other strategy.

Same picture. And it's amazing.

Someone walks up to it. "Wow... who took THAT picture?"

But this time, there isn't a business card next to it.

So suddenly... everyone is going up to the bride.

And it becomes that everyone is asking her, "Who is your photographer?"

Next thing you hear, "You know... I thought that was Gene Ho."

And this isn't just one guest. It's a ton of guests.

That's how you light up a room.

That's how you "use" a business card.

You use it sparingly.

So now you have the whole room a buzz talking about you.

And while you're at it?

If someone has an event coming up? They will come up to you - and it's THEN that you give them a business card.

If you're going to force business cards down people's throats like honey-roasted peanuts - your effect will be limited.

Consider the less-is-more route.

I do want to talk about an instance where leaving business cards out backfired for someone.

Here was the situation.

I had a bridal shoot for a bride.

The bride loved it. And I was pretty proud of it.

The bride even upgraded the picture to a large 20x30 canvas - complete with a custom frame.

So all is good. And my plan is working.

People are talking.

But here's where it went sour.

I was doing the photography, but the bride also hired a videographer.

I had no connection with this other video company.

They were quite nice actually.

But during the reception, they placed their business cards all over the venue.

And it's not my company - so I didn't care.

But the business card said "Wedding Videos - Wedding Photography" on it.

In other words… the bride hired them to do the wedding video. But they went with me to do the photography.

Granted - they didn't stick their cards anywhere near my bridal picture.

But I'm thinking about how many people got confused and thought those cards belonged to me.

It didn't bother me enough to say anything to them.

And I didn't think it was intentional.

But it's a good way to step on someone's toes. And at least the net result for them is that they probably wouldn't be a company I would recommend in the future.

Another thing this company did…

They put their cards next to the caterer's food set up.

I'm just thinking about how they feel with cards put on their table.

I know that if it was my catering company - that would rub me the wrong way.

If they asked permission to put their cards on their food set-up, that would be one thing.

But if they didn't and just left them there?

That would be no different if a caterer put their business cards on the edge of your engagement portrait.

Or imagine if it was the opposite.

Let's say that you own both a photography studio and a video company.

Actually… I have both.

My photography studio bears my name - and my video company is a sister company with its own name.

But let's say I have a business card that that says… Photography and Video.

(I don't… but if I did.)

If I was at that event and started leaving my cards all over the place…

I think the video company there would have the right to be upset.

Maybe not if someone asked me personally for a card.

But to leave it all over the place is a little different.

On the other hand --

I do know of photographers who have been quite crafty in their promotions.

I know of photographers who have made special "business cards" with the bride's picture on them. And they left them at each table.

I feel you. I think that's a great idea.

And I think that can be extremely effective.

My point is more that there are creative ways to use your business cards.

There are ways to make each card more effective then just throwing them out into the wind.

Chapter 9

Word of Mouth

Priceless.

Ultimately this is the goal of every photographer.

Word of Mouth is the lifeblood of what we do.

And in part? This is the key to effective marketing.

So how do you get it?

I will tell you.

But for starters... I'm not going to go into the twenty different things that you probably already know about.

There's so much you can just research on your own - or you can read about online.

Rather, I'm going to tell you the principle behind Word of Mouth.

Here we go...

Word of Mouth is nothing more than people talking about you.

It might be good. It might be bad.

But it's about getting people to talk about you and your photography work.

I'll address the part about the bad in a second.

In a minute I'm going to talk to you about how to handle the bad.

Because if you're marketing correctly. You will inevitably get both "good press" and "bad press."

I'll tell you how to deal with bad.

But let me tell you how to generate it in the first place.

OK...

Here is the secret to Word of Mouth.

You have to convince people that they own you.

What?!?

Yep.

I'll say it again and you can listen to me or ignore me.

You have to convince people that they own you.

Wow... what a statement, right?

Let me explain.

Do you know why I love Metallica?

Yes, Metallica. The band.

When I was in the tenth grade, I listened to Metallica's first album.

It was back in the days of cassette tapes.

Back then, their music was a little different. Definitely extreme for that era.

But I was listening to Metallica way before they ever got big.

Then one day, on their road to greatness... the band opened for some big group.

I can't remember who it was they opened for.

But while all my friends went to see the headline act... I was telling everyone about this amazing opening band.

Of course... in time, Metallica became a mega band.

But I have that connection to them.

Do I own them? No.

But I feel like I do.

I feel like I have this connection to them.

I love their music. I love what they do.

And I'm ready to jump into any conversation anyone might have that remotely involves heavy metal.

I've never met them.

But I feel a connection with them because I've listened to them from the start.

Now here is where we come in as photographers.

Word of Mouth builds with one fan at a time.

And each fan you get - each new client you get?

They have to be convinced you belong to them.

How that's done is up to you.

So how did I do it?

For me, I'm a servant that knows his master.

I'll explain that statement. But first a story.

I have a friend who is blind and has a guide dog.

The dog is incredible.

My friend walks near something dangerous and the dog barks.

If my friend drops his wallet on the ground, the dog stops and barks until he picks it up.

How is this possible?

The dog thinks that he owns my friend.

The dog was trained to think he owns the human.

OK… please understand the bigger picture here.

I'm not comparing my clients to a dog. Not in the least.

But my clients – they are fans of mine because they know I am here to serve them.

And I know them well.

My clients know they aren't a number to me.

In actuality… I know them more than they realize.

I feel indebted toward my clients.

And I appreciate them.

They are why I get to do what I do.

Two stories - both stock car related.

One I saw on TV and one personal.

When Dale Earnhardt, the famed NASCAR driver was still alive…

His son Dale, Jr. was just getting onto the scene.

I tried to look for this video clip on YouTube, but I couldn't find it.

But I remember seeing this live on TV as it was yesterday.

But Dale, Jr. just finished a race.

He was getting interviewed on live TV.

Then suddenly out of nowhere, Dale, Sr. comes into the TV frame.

He said, "Son... turn your hat around and show your sponsor."

Dale, Jr. was young at the time. And quite frankly... it was hip to turn your baseball cap backwards.

But he gets a lot of money to promote his sponsor.

So his Dad was telling him to acknowledge those who "got him there."

Ok... now for the second story.

This one is more personal.

I had sponsored a race car that runs in the ARCA series.

The driver was Jason Jarrett - the son of the famed NASCAR driver Dale Jarrett.

I was more than impressed and star struck that Jason would be driving a car that had the Gene Ho logo on it.

At this point, I never met Jason.

But I was in Chicago and talking to the team reps.

We were going over last minute specifics on the sponsorship.

That was when they asked me, "Do you want to talk to Jason?"

Of course I did.

So they called him up and put him on speaker phone.

"Jason... we have Gene Ho here. He's one of your sponsors."

And Jason's response?

"Yeah... I know Gene. I know who's on my car."

Geez. I tell you. That was an awesome feeling.

The point of all of this?

Love your clients.

Really do.

They are the reason why you're able to do what you LOVE to do.

Be in servitude to them.

Learn about them.

And watch your Word of Mouth grow.

Here's the lesson.

Word of Mouth DOES NOT come from your clients LEARNING ABOUT YOU.

It comes from YOU learning about THEM.

Once that happens?

Your Word of Mouth will be unstoppable.

Your fan base will feel a personal connection with you.

The ones you shot early on in your career?

They will love you even more.

After all... they were smart enough to figure out your talent before the rest of the world did.

Sort of like myself and Metallica.

I knew about them before the rest of the world did.

But as you build your studio?

Love your clients.

Be in servitude to them.

And they, in turn, will push you further.

Further than you ever imagined.

They will talk about you. They will promote you.

Just love them. Appreciate them. And never take them for granted.

OK… the "bad press" part.

Love it.

Learn to love opinions about you good or bad.

As long as you are doing a great job as a photographer.

As long as you treat people right.

As long as you respect those who make your job possible?

Then open your doors to bad Word of Mouth.

You can't make it unless you have it.

Believe me.

I want everyone to love me.

But it's just not possible.

There's no way.

Not everyone is going to love you.

Some of it might be authentic.

Maybe you had an off day and didn't do your best job shooting.

Or maybe it's a jealous competitor who spreads rumors about you.

Work at being the best photographer you can be.

But welcome criticism.

Because criticism is what sparks Word of Mouth.

Without criticism. Without rumors.

And quite frankly... without flat out lies about you - there is no true Word of Mouth.

Me personally?

My critics are good for me.

I've heard it all.

The good and the bad.

But I know who I am. I know what I do.

And what helps to fuel the Word of Mouth is the bad stuff.

Because it fosters discussion. And my fans come out in full force to defend me.

My fans... my clients... whom I serve.

Granted... I don't think you need to invent bad stuff about you.

We can all mess up on our own. And as we build our studio, there will no doubt be competitors who don't like us.

It's all good.

Because Word of Mouth comes from discussion - good or bad.

But your saving grace?

Build up your fan base.

Love them. And they will go to bat for you.

Now speaking of that?

Should you ever solicit Word of Mouth?

Should you ever tell your clients... your fan base... to promote you?

Yes and no.

As people talk about you - the good "press" will always do you well.

But very rarely do I ever ask someone to promote me.

Let's do it this way.

I'll turn it on you.

Next time you're at great restaurant.

The food is great.

You feel like you just ate a 3-piece Original Snack with Biscuit.

OK… joking.

But off subject. Who comes up with those names?

Funniest-ever chicken story.

I ate a meal once at this "chicken place."

So we get it straight - it wasn't KFC.

It was another company.

And I'm eating my lunch.

I finish eating this one piece of chicken and I'm looking at the bone.

And I say to my wife… "What in the world?"

But whatever it was… let's just say it was no discernable part of a chicken.

Seriously… we were looking that what I thought was a thigh. And that was no thigh bone.

I have no idea what that was.

OK… no lesson. No point.

But damn… fry it up and it's all good.

Ok… so my point about the restaurants…

When was the last time you went to a restaurant - and bragged about it because the waitress said, "Well y'all tell others about us."

Sure... you said, "Thank you! I will."

But do you really walk down the street and start talking about this great meal you just had?

For the most part - people talk about you or don't talk about you.

Point being?

If you want to generate word of mouth?

It certainly won't be because you asked your client to give you word of mouth.

Granted - you can ask them. And they may or may not follow through and actually talk about you.

The better strategy --

Maybe don't ask your clients talk about you.

How about you talk about THEM.

Interesting concept, huh?

How simple is that?

It's the basis of communication, but yet sometimes we only see things from one side: ours.

We want our clients to talk about us... so what? We ask them to?

No. The better way is to talk about them.

I'll show you how this is done.

I just finished a photo shoot with a model.

I find out that before she came to my studio - she got her hair done at the local salon.

"Cool... who was your hairdresser?" I ask.

She tells me and I know him.

Perfect.

I do the shoot. But next time I run into that hairdresser? I'm going to remember that shoot.

"Hey! I heard you did Cindy's hair for her shoot the other day. Wow… you did fantastic. I tell you… Cindy looked great. I have her pictures online now. I'll get the link out you."

The hairdresser gets the link. Sees the photos. Maybe even requests a few pictures for his portfolio.

And that's when it gets good.

"Sure… I tell you what. Can you ask Cindy if it's OK for me to give those photos to you?"

So the hairdresser talks to Cindy. And Cindy goes on and on about YOU.

Suddenly you are the topic of conversation.

That's how word of mouth is spread.

It starts with YOU talking.

If you think a simple, "Please tell other people that you liked our photos," will work?

Ask yourself if that's ever worked on you.

That's just not human nature.

But you tell me.

You're standing in line at the grocery store and you see your neighbor.

Now you tell me what your reaction would be if you heard this… (This is your neighbor talking to you…)

"Great to see you. You're not going to believe this. But last week we went to Jimmy's steakhouse for dinner. You left five minutes before I got in!"

See how that works?

What you would probably say?

"Oh yeah! You know Jimmy the owner? Wow. He is fantastic. And his food is incredible. Last week I went there and tried the blue cheese topped T-Bone. Incredible."

And what happens next?

Yep, you got it.

Before you know it, you're having a 10-minute conversation about this restaurant while you're waiting to buy your groceries.

How did this all come about?

Was it because Jimmy the restaurant owner said, "Hey! Please tell other people about me!"

No.

It was because Jimmy talked about you.

And it was because Jimmy authentically cares about his clients. His customers. His fan base.

Jimmy knows you. And he knows your neighbor.

He put two and two together - and quite frankly? He's just a down home good guy.

Your job is to be like Jimmy.

Know your clients. Know your fans.

And talk about them.

And in turn? They will talk about you.

Chapter 10

Free Milk and a Cow

At the time I was just dating my wife.

We weren't engaged yet. But we we'd been together for sometime.

We went to Wisconsin to visit her parents.

And while we were there, she started talking about cows.

Oh… OK. I get it.

I'm going to get this story about "free milk and a cow" and she wants a ring.

Well, that's what I thought.

Who knew.

She was really talking about actual cows. Literally cows.

So I got to visit with some cows that weekend at her family's farm.

Interesting factoid about cows.

For starters, the more you milk them - the more they produce.

And the second fact?

There really is no free milk.

I know that joke about "free milk and a cow" - is just that.

But even if you did own the cow - it's still not free.

You have to feed the cow. You have to care for it. You have to milk it.

At the very least - it takes time to milk a cow. At the most - it costs you to care for it.

And here's the point.

When it comes to your marketing dollars, I see a lot of photographers NOT investing in their own clients - and not calculating the COST of investing in their clients.

Now I'm not comparing my clients to cows.

But you get my vision.

When calculating your marketing budget - count in the time caring for your cows.

Your clients will give - and give more… if you milk them.

But it takes time.

And it SHOULD take money.

Money that you have to calculate into your marketing budget.

For starters, you have to give something back to your clients.

Granted, you can't give back fully to everyone.

But somehow you have to reward your BEST clients.

It could be by means of a free shoot. It could by means of a free 16x20.

Whatever. But you have to give back your best clients - the ones that really recommend you and bring you new clients.

Calculate that into your budget.

Story time.

This is long time ago. But way back when - I was using a particular album company.

The album company has already gone out of business and the studio has since moved on.

But back in the day, we were spending a lot of money buying wedding albums from this single company.

And it was legit.

We spent a ton of money with this company.

A ton.

And during Christmas time - they gave us a "thank you."

I wish I was joking. But we got a $10 gift certificate.

Trust me when I say we don't need to be thanked by the vendors we use.

All I ask with the lab we use and the vendors associated with our studio is a quality product and quite frankly - their ear.

If I'm spending an unusual amount of money with a company, I just ask to be respected.

So I don't really need any special gifts.

But I tell you… when you are literally spending tens of thousands of dollars with one company, and they thank you at Christmas time with a $10 gift certificate - it was more than offensive.

I hate to sound ungrateful, but I would rather have received nothing.

My current lab and album company, Black River Imaging out of Springfield, MO, has treated me with respect.

I don't need the gifts. But they gave me a gift when I got married.

And when I need something fast, they get it to me fast.

And there have been other companies that have treated me well for what I spend with them.

I've had companies that have offered me free passes to national conventions like PDN's PhotoExpo in New York.

I appreciate it all.

The point to this all is that you have to take care of your clients and especially the good ones.

And they are like me.

What they really want is great photography and the respect they deserve as my customer.

I'm not going to offend them and give them $5 off their next order of $100.

(Which by the way... you can now see how offensive a $10 gift certificate is after spending THOUSANDS with this one company. And to be fair, it might have been an accident - like a general mail out to all their clients - but still...)

But whenever possible - my studio budgets in our fair share of free shoots. Free 16x20 canvases.

We do it because we really do appreciate them.

But we also do it because I know nothing is really free.

It seems like a great thought to have a cash cow that keeps giving.

A cash cow that is recommending clients to you.

But appreciate that and give back.

And give back from your marketing budget.

I don't have a rule of thumb.

I guess that's for you to figure out.

Like I can't say, "Take 10% of your ad budget and put that back into taking care of your best clients."

If I had to guess?

I'd say that might be the case.

But at the same time, the most valuable thing I can give them is my time.

So we do a lot of free shoots.

I think you need to.

And I do realize that it's a hard thing to do.

Our value is our artistic ability.

But I think that's why it means so much to our clients.

They know what we're worth.

So maybe give that back.

But count it.

Count it in your marketing budget.

To give what I said more credibility, do this.

Ask one of your fellow pro photographers, "How much did you spend on advertising this year?"

Lets say they throw out a very reasonable number for a one-man show. That is a single photographer working by themselves.

$5,000.

Perfect.

Now ask them how they spent that number.

If they say, "I spent $2,000 in bridal shows and $1,000 on online ads and $2,000 on a magazine ad."

OK... then you now know they really don't get the full picture.

They are not considering their hidden costs.

I don't doubt for a minute that photographer is successful.

But consider your true costs.

That advertising money should go "both ways."

That is... it goes back to what I talked about earlier.

What is your **Gross Marketing Impact**.

It should account for both the paid and the unpaid.

And even within the paid? It should for all the stuff that you don't consider.

If the number was indeed $5,000 on advertising.

Then it would be more realistic if it were the following.

Question:

How much did you spend in advertising last year?

Answer:

I spent $20,000 last year.

OK...

I don't encourage making up stuff.

But please understand the principle here.

The real discussion? Or at least if they read this book?

Then that means only $5,000 was spent on paid ads, but the actual Gross Marketing Impact was $20,000.

And yes, now you know...

Answer:

My **Gross Marketing Impact** *was actually $20,000.*

I did well this year.

I managed to trade out $8,000 with this amazing deal with this radio station.

It was had work, but I did all their headshots and shot candid photos at their Christmas party.

But I got $8,000 worth of commercials for it.

I also spent $1,000 on these great new rate cards.

This year, I spent $2,000 on sample albums for my studio.

I did spend $2,000 on bridals shows.

And I spent $1,000 on online ads.

Crazy... I took a gamble and paid $2,000 in a magazine ad. But I think it was well worth it.

I think it was.

I also spent $2,000 on gift cards.

I gave them away to a few charities to auction off.

And actually? I sold 5 of them personally at $200 each, so I made out well.

To top it off... I sent $2,000 back to my clients.

Yeah... I gave away a few free shoots. But it was to my good clients.

If you can believe it?

One of my clients referred four weddings to me.

So I did give away a free 16x20 canvas print to her.

I also gave away a few other photo shoots.

Two of them, if you can believe it.

I just did the shoot and gave them the disk hi-res.

But they were worth it. They personally spent $5,000 each with me this year - so I thought it was well worth it.

See how that works?

There are two answers.

The easier answer is $5,000.

The answer that you and I now understand is $20,000 as our Gross Marketing Impact.

The REAL answer?

$5,000 in real world dollars

$2,000 in gifts to my clients.

$8,000 in trades

$3,000 in studio promo pieces.

$2,000 in gift certificates/promotions

That was what was really spent.

Chapter 11

The Paid Ads - The "When and Where" - and How Much

However you lay it down - it's hard to grow without spending real word dollars on real world ads.

I will tell you my whole strategy on this.

But let me start with the main thing... how much?

How much should you spend?

If you pick up most books on marketing, the suggested number is about 10 percent of your gross income.

For easy math sake - I agree with that number.

But here's where the mistakes I've made in the past come into play.

Again... for easy math sake:

Let's say that your studio grosses $100,000 a year.

That is a healthy number for a one or two person studio.

So if you take 10 percent of that? Your marketing budget is at $10,000.

Here is where the danger comes in.

If you spend $10,000 in buying ads, and your studio grosses $100,000?

You will soon find yourself in trouble.

That is because in that $10,000 - most people don't include all the other factors that also include money.

If you spend $2,000 on show books, $1,000 on new studio displays, $500 on new rate cards, $1,000 on a bridal show and… then you spend $10,000 on a magazine ad?

Guess what? Your budget is now over by $4,500.

Do your math and stick to it.

If your marketing budget is $10,000.

You want your Gross Marketing Impact to be $40,000.

But you want your actual "Ad Buying Dollars" to be about $5,000.

Out of that budget of 10 percent… you have to reserve part of that for NON-AD marketing.

Business Cards. Rate Cards. Show Books.

You have to include all of that into your budget.

I hope that makse sense. Marketing in three sections: paid ads, non-paid advertising (rate cards, etc.) and your estimated number, the value of your trades - your Gross Marketing Impact.

Now you see how photographers addicted to marketing - like me… can get into trouble.

Imagine me with a big marketing budget.

I'm looking at my gross revenues.

Wow… look at me! I should have 10 percent set aside to buy ads!

No... that's not the case.

And that's where the trouble begins.

For easy math... take a company that is just kicking butt.

The studio is making $1 million a year.

You think it would be wise to buy $100,000 worth of ads?

That's where the trouble begins.

Sure. You can do that.

But what are you going to print your rate cards on? Toilet paper?

Before you know it, that company would be overwhelmed.

Spending $100,000 gross of $1 million would paralyze a company.

Because the everyday marketing has to account for a larger portion of that dollar amount.

I hate to ever just specify numbers.

I hate to set rules.

Because everyone and every company is different.

But here are my target numbers.

The marketing dollars should still be at 10 percent.

But of those marketing dollars, the actual percentage reserved for PAID ads should be:

0 percent for up to $29,999

2 percent from $30,000 to $49,999.

5 percent from $50,000 and above.

And again... this is based on the annual GROSS from the year before.

OK, please let me explain and justify my numbers.

Let's say you're a start up.

You're doing well. You're getting some good shoots.

For easy math, let's say last year you made $10,000 gross. And so now you're setting your marketing budget for next year.

I believe that your marketing budget should STILL be 10 percent.

But that 10 percent should NOT be spent on paid advertising.

I believe you should take out $1,000 to buy rate cards and business cards to have money for trades.

$1,000 to do that is a nice amount.

What CAN'T happen is that photographer spending $1,000 in ads.

Because you can't do that and still buy business cards.

But should that photographer spend 5% of that on ads?

I would say no.

But the reason being?

$500 isn't really enough to have THAT much of an impact.

It would be better to spend ALL of that on non-traditional marketing.

$500 invested in the HARD COST of some trades could potentially give you thousands to add to your Gross Marketing Impact target.

But spending $500 on ads at that time would have little impact.

Once you get into the $30,000 range, a real chance for some impact.

At that point? 2% set aside for real world advertising - spending real world dollars would be at $600

With that? A wedding photographer could buy a bridal show.

Or even a halfway decent mailing list for high-school seniors.

Granted, at $600, those dollars are still limited

But remember... that's your REAL WORLD dollars spent on advertising.

At $30,000 you're managing a 10 percent - $3,000 budget.

That means $2,400 of that should be utilized in non-traditional marketing. Rate Cards. Business cards. Show books.

So you're still spending money. Just not all of it on paid advertising.

If I had to put numbers to it:

About $50,000 a year gross is the real turning point.

That's why I had it down for the jump to 5 percent.

Yes. At this point you're still spending 10 percent in marketing.

But you are not spending $2,500 on "other stuff."

And now you are controlling $2,500 worth of dollars to spend on ads.

That's a lot.

And that is a number that can have some impact.

All right.

At this point - I realize that there is a difference between rule of thumb - and sheer business instinct.

Me personally?

At times I feel like I'm at a roulette table in Reno.

That's my biggest weakness and yet my biggest strength.

I see opportunities in advertising and I salivate.

I see a bridal show coming up. And I'm way past my budget as it is.

But I say, "You know what? It's only $700. All I have to do is book a wedding from it and I make my money back and more."

Or... I might have an opportunity to put a magazine ad in a prominent location - say a back page.

"I can do it," I think to myself.

I stick that ad there and I'll get make my money back easy.

That's how I am.

I naturally take chances.

So when you look at the numbers here, you'll see my personal rule of thumb.

Know that I fight that every step of the way.

I know what's good for me. I know what I need to do.

But I fight that every step of the way.

And I've been doing halfway decent with that.

In time's past, I've been like a drunken gambler when it came to my ad dollars.

But I would have to say the numbers I set here are pretty accurate.

OK... that being said.

Let me talk a little bit about the "when and where" of ads.

Basically, WHAT to buy and more importantly WHEN.

Most photographers when they talk to me, will ask me about WHAT to buy.

In other words, what is greater? Google Ad words or a Yellow Page ad?

Which is greater? A magazine ad or a bridal show?

I guess we can start by talking about WHAT to buy first.

Then let's talk about the more important part - the WHEN.

Here's the "what" part.

The easy answer to this is that there are very few limitations on the "what" part.

At the start of this book, I was talking about how it used to be simple.

It used to be an ad in the yellow pages.

That was what you spend your money on - end of story.

Here's the funny part of it.

I'll go more into this in a little bit with the "when" part.

But right now? It might now be a bad time to go back into the yellow pages.

When I first started my studio? You could go to "photographers" in the yellow pages and it was pages and pages of listings and ads.

There were big full-page ads. There were small 1/8 page display ads.

Today? You go to your yellow pages and there are just a few pages (if that) of photographer listings.

Here's my point.

I don't think you can say right now that yellow page advertising has not become irrelevant.

I haven't done one in a long time.

But I would certainly consider one.

I haven't checked what a half page ad costs.

Let's say that 10 years ago it costs $1,000 a year.

But 10 years ago - say everyone was still using the yellow pages.

And say you were a medium-sized studio.

So your $1,000 half-page ad is not in the midst of eight-pages of photographers.

Some who are spending $2,000 for full-page ads. Some who are spending $3,000 for full-page - full color ads.

How effective would that $1,000 ad be?

And thus, the point being?

Right now the yellow pages are so bare.

All the photographers have their money elsewhere.

So right now, a half page ad in they yellow pages might DOMINATE the whole section.

Am I doing it now? No.

Would I consider it?

Most definitely.

It's kind of like stocks.

When I first started getting involved with investing money and the stock market, my mom told me something very interesting.

She said, "When everyone is talking about it, it's already too late."

Think about how that applies to us in marketing as photographers.

I mentioned this only because at the time of me writing this book, there is virtually no buzz about yellow page advertising.

Sorry for the industry, but there just isn't.

At the same time? I've seen all the "hot" places to advertise.

In the past? Some of these online wedding places were huge.

I'm not saying it doesn't work.

It has worked VERY well in the past.

I'm sure it's still working very well now.

My point being, if EVERYONE buys into it? How effective can it POSSIBLY BE?

That being said…

I've tried about everything.

All of it.

Movie Theatres

Race Cars

Yellow Pages

Magazines

Bridal Shows

Billboards

Direct Mail

Online Advertising

If you can think of a few more - I bet I've tried it.

Rather than give you a play-by-play on what I think of each "type" of paid advertising.

What I would like to do is tell you what I'm currently doing.

And then I'd like to discuss the more important issue - that is WHEN you're doing it.

Currently, here is how my paid advertising dollars are being spent.

50% in Bridal Shows.

25% in Billboards.

25% in Magazine.

First, I'll give my explanation on why these are my current choices.

My studio is primarily a wedding photography studio.

That is what we specialize in.

I like Bridal Shows because it gives us one-on-one time with the brides.

Is it "the be-all and the end-all"?

No.

No way.

In a given area, if I had to place where we received most of our weddings?

At least 50 percent is still good Ol' Fashioned Word of Mouth.

And I bet I'm being conservative about that 50 percent number.

And also… as mentioned earlier in this book. That "Word of Mouth" doesn't happen by accident.

But I still feel we do reach a good amount of brides through bridal shows.

Is it 50 percent worth?

No way. Not even close.

But there's a reason why we still do bridal shows.

Bridal shows put us in touch with other vendors.

There have been times when my studio was virtually sold out.

When I say, virtually sold out?

What I mean is that most KEY dates are sold out.

You could be a one-photographer studio and be virtually sold out with 30 weddings a year.

But you always hope for that "weird wedding date" - may be the rare Friday wedding.

But there have been times where my studio was virtually sold out.

But I still bought a bridal show.

Why would I do that?

Why would I buy a $700 bridal show when technically I don't need it?

Because that's the Art of Marketing.

It's because I'm MARKETING and not advertising.

Yes.

If I'm sold out, or "virtually" sold out…

I hope to go into that bridal show and book a Tuesday wedding in December.

Chances are? That's not going to happen.

But… that $700 I just spent on a bridal show?

That money isn't being spent on getting a new wedding.

That money is spent to market myself.

Granted. I understand.

Everyone has to watch their budget and I'm not so big that I can afford to spend advertising money when I'm already sold out.

But what I'm saying is that money spent has a PURPOSE.

The purpose might be to get new clients NOW… or it can be spent on getting new clients LATER.

OK… here's the example of why I would spend $700 on a bridal show when I know I'm already sold out.

If I'm already sold out, there's a good chance that we're going to go into that show and meet a lot of our brides.

The purpose of that $700 spent is NOT to market to new brides. The purpose of that $700 is to market to my fellow VENDORS.

In other words, I'm not marketing to my fellow vendors so that LATER on, that they will return good for good.

This is how it works.

We're at a bridal show, and we run into one of our brides.

Here's the conversation:

"Hey! Julie. Great to see you. How's all the planning going?"

Then she's filling us in on all the details.

"Huh… really? Still haven't found a florist? OK… I tell you what. I'm taking a break in just about two minutes. How about we go over to one of the florists I know and let me introduce you."

Ah… you see?

Do you feel me?

Do you see the power you have and the power you wield as a photographer?

That florist? Once they get that job? How much will they love you?

My secret in this regard is that not all of your paid advertising has to be targeting new clients.

Sometimes it should be targeted to targeting your fellow vendors to get clients LATER ON.

And that's where the "when" comes in.

Everyone talks about WHAT to advertise with.

The better question is WHEN to advertise.

OK…

Here's the situation.

Let me tell you when I use magazine ads and when I don't.

I live in in Myrtle Beach, SC.

That is where my home studio is.

There are many good photography studios there.

But honestly, my return on a magazine advertising would be limited.

Not to say I wouldn't do a magazine ad here.

All I'm saying is that I have a foothold here.

Simple enough.

If I did a magazine ad here, it would be great and wonderful, but I'm not sure how effective it would be.

OK…

Now about 90 miles down the road is another city.

But three years ago, we wanted to increase our presence there.

In this case… the timing was right. The WHEN of it.

Here's why.

So you know… I spent $2,000 or so for a full-page ad in a bridal magazine there.

Why spend it there?

The timing was right.

There were two reasons.

And if you can grasp the WHY of this? And you can train yourself to understand it?

Then you will start to get the heartbeat of marketing - at least as a pro photographer.

At the time? My studio was just starting to get established in that area.

We were doing tons of weddings already - but we wanted a stronger foothold.

We were already doing bridal shows there.

But we wanted a bigger presence.

An opportunity came about in one of the bridal magazines.

Prime real estate as I call it.

The back-page of the magazine came up.

This was my opportunity.

I bought that back page.

The reason?

The timing was right.

Of course... the first reason was that the back page came open.

If there's a good magazine, getting the back page isn't easy.

Not all the time, but usually... the person that gets the back page keeps it until they decide not to renew.

So the opportunity came about.

We were there - the right time and the right place.

And we got the back page.

So that was one of the WHEN "points" that came in handy.

The other point?

The other "when" part is that we needed a bigger presence.

We needed a statement that we weren't fly-by-night.

That we were there. And we were there to stay.

Very few things work better than a magazine ad on the back page to express that.

And it wasn't necessarily targeted to the brides there.

I put that magazine ad there to target the other vendors.

I put it there so that the other vendors would know, "Hey. It's OK. I'm investing money here. I'm not going anywhere anytime soon. So please recommend me to your clients."

That is a big part of the "when."

Part of the secret to marketing is knowing WHEN to use WHAT tool.

If you refer back to the FONT chapter in this book - it's the same principle.

OK... say I'm in Myrtle Beach.

This is a big tourist town.

Normally speaking... and quite frankly - when I said before that there were very few forms of paid advertising I didn't try?

Well here is one.

In Myrtle Beach, there are a lot of pancake houses.

When you go there to get some eggs, you sit down to this paper place mat.

There - you will find all kinds of advertising.

You would normally never find me putting my logo there.

Mostly? I don't want to advertise my high-end photo studio next to ads for "Dragon Putt-Putt Golf" and half price bikini waxing.

Would there ever be a time when I would want to advertise on a paper place mat?

I'm sure.

Maybe if I wanted to aggressively go after the family beach portrait business.

But then again - I'm currently running a "prestige" marketing campaign.

At the same time, I am an equal opportunity moneymaker.

Me personally? I love honest photography work.

I love what I'm doing now. But if the direction of my studio turned so I needed to make a living doing hi-volume beach shoots - I could live with that.

And if that was the case, you could see how the "tone" of my marketing campaign would change. How the fonts would change. How my ad placement would change.

It's a matter of "when."

Or better said… a matter of timing.

An ad in a pancake house right now would hurt the image of my studio.

But I could see myself using it earlier on in my career.

When I first started photography - I wasn't doing a whole lot of weddings.

And I wasn't prestigious.

But I needed the cash flow to get my studio up and running.

Way back when, I used to do a lot of dance school photos.

I would go to the jazz, tap and ballet schools… set up shop, and shoot away.

As a young studio, it was a great way kick up the cash flow.

If I thought about it? An ad in a pancake house might have done me well back then.

Referring back to that point earlier about Yellow Page ads.

The timing MIGHT be right to get back into it.

Would I get high-end brides from it?

That's debatable.

But being that I live in a destination area --

Let me give you an idea how another photographer can out play me.

And here's where my honesty and candor comes out.

I'm telling other photographers how to beat me.

In Myrtle Beach, I have a big presence.

So let's say there was a destination wedding here.

A bride that lives in Ohio is getting married in Myrtle Beach because her mom lives here. Or... perhaps she grew up here and already knew about me.

But she's in Ohio and says, "Mom... can you get me the number for Gene Ho? I want to hire him for my wedding."

So mom pulls out the yellow pages and searches for my name.

I don't advertise at all in the yellow pages - but I do get my free listing in there.

Her mom writes down my number. But meanwhile, she sees your ad.

Your ad is amazingly prominent because right now there's not a whole lot of big ads in there right now.

So she sees your big ad and she also writes your number down - and maybe even your website.

So she tells her daughter... "I got Gene Ho's number here. Here it is. But just in case he's not available... I also have this other studio."

Suddenly the bride's interest is piqued and she checks you out. She falls in love with your work - and you just scored a big win over me.

See how this all comes in to play?

Not that it's all about targeting me - but it can go for any other studio as well.

It's just that at one time, it was very hard to dominate the yellow pages.

But now it's not as hard.

OK... to finish off this discussion of WHEN...

I'll give you two examples of times when I messed up in my timing.

Not everything I've done in my life has always been great and wonderful.

Actually, that's the furthest from the truth.

I tell people openly that my career is based upon a foundation of failure.

I hate failing.

I hate messing up.

But I'm pretty good at picking myself up and fixing my mistakes.

The following two examples are mistakes I've made.

They're mistakes that you can learn from.

And when you read about it, you might think, "Big deal? That's a small mistake."

But that's the point.

Small "victories" shape your career.

Basically, you build you career one victory at a time. One great shoot at a time and you string them together over many weeks... months... years.

I don't think you can look back at my career and point to this or that as the one monumental turning point.

Mostly, I've built my career with small steps.

But it's the same for my mistakes.

A few "small" mistakes - strung together, can destroy your business.

Also... I don't count my calculated gambles as mistakes.

Not everything I do is going to succeed.

But part of the American Dream is that you have a right to gamble on yourself.

You have the right to take risks on your talent - on your own skill.

So I don't count calculated risks as a mistake.

If I have a good feeling that "this or that" marketing campaign might succeed? I'm willing to take a risk on it.

And if I fall flat on my face, I can more than live with that.

But here are two mistakes - regarding timing... the "when."

And these were authentic mistakes.

Timing Mistake #1 - Staying at the Table Too Long

One thing I do feel great about?

I have a great sense of opportunity.

I see opportunity very clearly.

I don't remember the exact time.

It was fairly early on in my career.

While I wasn't a start-up anymore, I was at the point where it was debatable of whether I was a truly making an impact in the wedding industry.

At the time, there really wasn't any bridal magazine in the area.

There were the "newspaper" variety - but there wasn't really a full-color glossy.

So me, trying to stay on top of the industry --

I see this new magazine coming about.

And so did the whole city.

Not that I could remember... but we really never had anything like this.

So I jumped on the opportunity.

But ONLY if I could get the back page.

For me? It wasn't really about reaching the brides.

It was about making a statement to the other wedding vendors.

I was saying, "Hey... I'm here. I have the back page. And you're right. I've been doing real well and booking a lot of brides. So please help me and I'll send my clients your way."

I got that back page and I really think it helped solidify what I was trying to do here in my hometown.

OK... and now for my thoughts about staying at the table too long.

Staying at the table too long is a reference used in Las Vegas and Reno.

In other words - you get lucky. You win some hands.

But you think it's all going to last forever.

And you just stay there too long.

Before you know it? Your big win is neutralized by your losses.

I really did well way back when by getting that back page ad.

It was a gutsy move on my part and it worked.

The timing was right and I moved fast enough - and put up enough money - to get that back page.

The ad had a lot of impact and it went to reassure everyone that indeed... I was a player in this industry.

Now fast forward a handful of years.

The ad did its intended purpose.

But I kept the ad too long.

Way too long.

The ad fulfilled its purpose.

And in THIS case, the ad was NOT to target brides. It was specifically there to target VENDORS.

It was there to make a statement.

A back-page ad in any magazine is very pricey.

Could I have justified that the ad got me some brides that booked?

You can debate that all day long.

In other words, did the cost of the ad MAKE me money by getting new brides to sign up?

Maybe yes. Maybe no.

But I think no. But here's why.

The magazine was mainly distributed at bridal shows.

Bridal shows where we already bought a booth.

If I was a home-studio photographer, it might have been a good idea for me have that back page ad.

I might have needed that back page ad to made a statement I was, indeed established, even though I was home-based.

But there was no question I was established NOW... that is YEARS after the ad ran the first time.

I already had a brick and mortar studio and most everyone in town knew me.

But instead, year after year, this back page ad drained my account.

Again...

Not to say that the ad didn't work.

What I'm saying is the ad ALREADY fulfilled its purpose - that is getting the attention of other vendors.

The debate now becomes - could the money spent on this ad be BETTER SPENT on other things?

On top of all of it, this ad (renewed year after year) was bought during the time when I went on a grand advertising spending spree.

The lesson learned is this:

When you choose to pay for advertisement... ESTABLISH THE PURPOSE of that advertisement.

By the way, I'm not a gambler at the casinos.

I have put some money in the slots in my time.

But it's really not my thing.

At the same time, I'm using a casino analogy here.

It's kind of like someone going to the craps table and winning $1,000.

And he feels really good about everything.

And he says, "You know what? This is great. I just won $1,000. But I'm going to sit here and play until I lose $250."

Basically, you did well. You won $1,000. But you're not going to be stupid. And even if you start losing - you're still walking away with $750.

The point being?

Sometimes you go with your gut feeling.

And that's good.

That's why it's called, "The ART of Marketing" and not, "The TECHNICAL SKILLS of Marketing."

Marketing is still an art form.

It's about ebb and flow. It's about feel.

Granted, there are some really neat principles to follow.

And that's what I'm telling you about in this book.

But when you trust your gut feeling and go out on a limb.

And you actually WIN.

And your marketing campaign goes well.

Know when to leave well enough alone.

Even when things work, at least DEBATE whether that same money can be more effective spent elsewhere.

Maybe yes. Maybe no.

But at least debate it.

That's what I didn't do.

Add to that a couple of more mistakes and before you know it?

Before you know it… I got myself into a cash flow problem.

Not good.

Timing Mistake #2 - Know the Season

It's in the Bible.

"For everything there is a season."

But what separates the smart from the dumb?

Yep. You probably recognize that.

I didn't.

Here's the story.

The fundamental truth for most - if not ALL of us professional photographers...

We are like farmers.

There's a time to sow. There's a time to reap.

In short, we have strong months and weak months. Bright seasons and thick floods.

And you probably already know when that is.

I know I will make more money in May than I will in January.

And oddly... I have a friend that is not a photographer - but a graphic designer.

He says that he earns more in January than May.

That's because in January, all business are redoing their business cards - their brochures.

That is HIS season.

By May... no one is thinking about updating their promo material. They are too busy working.

So that is how his season goes.

Your season is different.

My season is different.

I'm primarily a wedding photographer.

So I spend most of January just picking up retainer checks for weddings later in the year.

Realizing that is key.

So here was the situation.

The month was May.

And one of my billboards was coming up for renewal.

Being one to always look for an opportunity, I found another billboard - one at a more prominent location.

All good.

Here was the problem.

The better location also cost more. It was $400 more than the old one.

I could debate myself all day long if it was worth it.

But I was making good money. It was May!

So decided to make the change.

OK… that's the first "maybe" mistake.

Maybe because it may or may not have been worth it to upgrade to a better location.

But here's the real mistake.

When I decided to move locations, I decided to change out my billboard design.

That's a good idea.

But what I didn't notice, was that this new board was slightly "thinner"

So when I designed the new billboard, I used the same dimensions of the OLD billboard.

This old billboard was just 2 feet taller than the new one.

In other words… I goofed in the design by 2 feet on the height.

The funny part is that I designed it in Photoshop, so the mistake was actually 2 inches too high.

So when I submitted the design, the billboard company told me I had a choice.

I could either: a) redo the design. Or b) buy the extra 2 feet worth of extension.

And by the way… 2 feet worth of extensions sounds like nothing.

But in actuality, it's 2 feet multiplied by the length.

If the billboard is 2 feet higher… then the extension (that is the actual wood they have to add on to the billboard) is actually 2 x 40 feet (the width of the billboard.).

Um… that's not cheap.

The thing is?

There's no real impact difference.

Sure… the billboard would be slightly bigger. But the impact is the same.

The only way you could justify it, is if it were a "weird" extension.

Like some business will use extensions and they will have things "popping out" of the billboard.

For instance, a golf course billboard might have the end of a golf club "sticking out" of the billboard as an extension.

I wasn't doing that.

I was simply going from a rectangle design - to a slightly bigger rectangle design.

So you can now guess what happened.

It was May. I was in the midst of my busy season.

I was making a lot of money.

I not only agreed to a more expensive location.

I also was too lazy to redesign the billboard.

So I told them just to add on the extension and pass the extra "rent" cost to me.

Between the old board and the new "better" location.

And between the old board and the new "extensions," that new billboard suddenly cost double.

Thing was?

I could afford it… in May.

But the season changed.

And suddenly, the great idea in May… and my laziness in May… added up. I paid for it later in January.

What I could afford in the busy season, I couldn't afford in the slow season.

When considering WHAT you're going to do – consider the timing.

Consider the season.

Granted, this mistake wasn't as bad.

I realized the mistake faster this time.

But in this case, I took an opportunity and neutralized it.

With this mistake - I could have utilized my resources much better.

Chapter 12

Branding and How it's Done

You hear that word a lot - branding.

Businesses talk about branding all the time.

Just what is branding and how does it apply to your career as a photographer?

Again… full disclosure. I don't have a lot of formal business training.

I don't have an MBA. And I don't know a lot about business outside the photography realm.

So I don't really know much about the proper definition of it.

Sure. I just "Googled" it… but that's the point.

Branding is when the public is so conscience of you that you are to wedding photography as "Google" is to "internet word search."

That is a "tall order."

And that's why I'd like to start my discussion with Starbucks.

I've been a Starbucks addict for quite some time now.

Right now, they own the consciousness of America.

I can be driving down the road and I see that green sign and it beckons me to get a cup.

My order is very simple.

It's a tall coffee, sugar-free hazelnut. Two Splenda and one cream.

I'm famous in Myrtle Beach for sending interns to the local Starbucks to pick up my coffee.

And it's always impressive to the interns that before they rattle off the words, "...sugar free hazel..." - the Starbucks Barista says, "...for Gene?"

It's my drink.

Going back a few chapters when I talked about, "owning a company?"

I feel like I own Starbucks.

I don't.

I don't even own stock in it.

But I feel like I do. And I'm a fan of Starbucks.

What Starbucks has managed to do, is brand their company in an amazing way.

Here's a simple test.

Next time you're at Starbucks... say this...

"Um... yeah. I'd like to have a cup of coffee. Make it a Suprema. And I'd like some of those chocolate covered graham crackers."

I don't know why I think that's so funny.

But Starbucks has three sizes.

It's Tall, Grande and Venti.

I love it.

They have single handedly changed our consciousness.

What in the world is a Suprema?

I have no idea.

It doesn't exist.

But neither does Venti.

Since when has Venti become synonymous with LARGE.

Tall is the small coffee. Grande is the medium. And Venti is the extra large.

Or if you want to confuse the Barista (yes… the coffee person) - then you can say the Suprema.

But for now… Starbucks has successfully branded themselves.

Speaking of which…

Just so annoying.

But I had a girlfriend one time that just loved to show off her incredibly complex Starbucks drink order.

Just so annoying.

"Um… I'd like a Grande Mocha Latte Machiado Chimicago with Steamed Goat Milk and Espresso Dip…"

It used to drive me crazy.

Especially when she would ask me to order.

It's like, "Dude… I have no idea what that is! Help me out here."

OK… my girlfriend wasn't a dude - but you get the point.

It drove me crazy.

But the Baristas at Starbucks would know exactly what it was and get it for her every time.

So I'm sure you get my point.

How powerful can your studio become when you have entered the consciousness of your clients?

My question to you? Are you branding your studio?

Often imitated…

But for the longest time, I've had four wedding packages.

Elite. Heritage. Prestige. Platinum.

I love it.

It's especially funny when photographers copy the scheme and replace my words with "like minded" words.

All good.

I don't mind it at all.

But that's a basic concept of branding - which is naming your products.

One of my friends who owned his own studio was commenting on my naming structure.

And we were joking about similar packages.

The highest package being called something amazing like, "The Caribbean Destination."

And the lowest package being called the, "Barefoot, Pregnant… Shotgun."

Naming your packages is just the start.

But we've also named a few of our products.

Right now… we have a product we call the "Fusion Album."

Basically, it's what most people would call a "Flush Mount Album" or a "Magazine Album."

You all know what I'm talking about.

But we call it a Fusion Album.

And I love it when brides refer their friends to us and they refer to this album as the Fusion Album.

Sometimes they call it the Suprema Album.

No... just kidding.

But my point being...

Brand. Build a brand.

Think about ways to be different.

Think of ways to stand out.

At my studio - my photographers always wear black to weddings.

I realize that I'm not the first photographer to ever wear black.

But I happen to like the color black.

On any given day, I'm usually wearing black.

I've been asked before what the reason is.

One of the reasons?

Black is one of the few colors that you can wear that you can be both "formal and casual" at the same time.

I don't like to wear neckties.

Not at all.

And if I wear black - I'm formal - but yet I don't have to be formal.

Anyway... that's part of the reason.

But my photographers have always worn black at weddings.

We call it "Gene Ho Blacks."

And we go to weddings in pairs.

So it becomes a nice trademark when you see two photographers at a wedding wearing black.

Do other studios do the same thing?

Of course.

Am I the first studio to do that?

Who knows.

But we've been doing this for a long, long time.

And I know that way before when…

Most of the wedding photographers would wear a tuxedo to the weddings.

I'm not into tuxedos.

I think they look amazing.

It's just not me.

So we wear black.

And it's part of what we do.

The idea behind it is, that we as a studio are branding an image.

If you want to put this to a test.

Next time you're shopping, go to the nearest $15 dollar haircut place.

Look at the hair stylists there and see how they are dressed.

Next. Find a beauty salon.

A high-end place. Maybe one where the haircut is in the $50 range.

How are they dressed?

Actively brand your image by how you look.

It's part of marketing.

Chapter 13

Connect the Dots

One of the highest forms of marketing is connecting the dots.

This part is truly an art form.

And that's why I love talking about this.

And this is why marketing really fascinates me.

Ultimately, marketing is about getting people to talk about you.

If you can visualize it... think about marketing as one big connect-the-dot drawing.

The big mistake is thinking you need to finish your drawing by connecting the dots from point A to point B for your client.

That is flawed thinking.

And if you can understand this concept, then you're well on your way to success.

The truth of it is that between A and B... there is actually A.a - A.b - A.c and then B.

And in actuality?

You really don't want to go directly from A to B.

You want as MANY "dots" along the way.

The more dots you have along the way? The more effectively you have marketed yourselves.

Everyone thinks it goes from A to B.

No.

That is the most rudimentary form of marketing.

That is what happens at bridal shows.

We show up. We meet the brides.

We go from A to B.

Some photographers take it to a level one step up from that.

Then go from A to A.a to B.

A.a being another vendor - say the florist.

That is a better form of marketing because A.a can tell several people about you.

Senior photographers have also done this.

My studio doesn't do a lot of senior photos. But I know how it works.

A lot of photographers have senior reps. The senior reps then become the "dot" to the client.

What you want in your marketing program is to create the most "dots" between A and B.

It's the complete opposite of what you would think.

You THINK it would want to go directly to the potential client.

In fact, you have some forms of advertising that claim they are reaching DIRECTLY to your potential client base.

Some direct mail companies say that.

And I'm certainly not knocking a whole industry.

Some of them claim that they "…only mail out to the most influential neighborhoods!"

OK… all good.

And it may or may not work.

But that's the point.

There's not real formula in business.

We're talking about marketing as an ART FORM.

Ideally, what you want is as many dots between A and B as possible.

If you have just one, you are about average.

If you have two? You're doing better.

Try to create five dots.

Try to create five people in between you and your prospective and eventual client.

First of all… why is that good?

Why is connecting the dots more superior than going directly to your prospective client?

OK…. This whole book boils down to this point here.

That is because the more people in between YOU and your prospective client - the MORE they talk about you.

Ta Dah!!!

Lets see this in action.

You are a senior photographer.

You meet a high school senior and you tell her. "Hey! Yeah. I'm a photographer. I can do a great job on your senior photos. We can go to the lake… do some really neat stuff!"

Wow... that is some fantastic marketing, right?

OK. But you take it one step further.

You get a senior rep. And you do a great job taking some sample photos of her.

Suddenly she's telling everyone about you.

The more people you can get between you and your eventual client the better.

OK... now let me show you how this works in real life.

And like I mentioned before.

I really can't give you a step by step per se.

There really are no "right ways" to do this or "checklists" of things to do.

But understand the concept and try to master it.

Let me show you how I've done this in one instance.

My flagship studio is in Myrtle Beach, SC.

Because we process orders there from our other locations, we do a lot of volume with shipping.

We have become famous at our shipping location of choice. Mostly because we do a lot of shipping at the end of the day.

More than anything, I think we annoy them.

Think about the crew there getting ready to finish up their day.

Meanwhile, we come in at the last minute with a bunch of boxes we need shipped.

We do this day after day.

And with this, I see an opportunity to create some new "dots."

The crew at my shipping location may or may not ever use my photo services.

But to me, that doesn't matter one bit.

Besides them being authentically nice people. Really... we put them through a lot coming in at the last minute all the time.

But they are a potential "dot."

So every once in a while, I make an investment of $8 to convert them into a dot.

My investment of choice?

Krispy Kreme donuts.

Every once in a while, I'll send the studio intern in with a bunch of boxes... and a box of Krispy Kreme.

It's amazing how a donut can shape public opinion of you.

The idea is first of all - to work to be a nice and appreciative person.

But it's truly amazing how a donut can get people to talk about you.

The clerk eats the donut.

She goes home and tells her husband how our studio did a nice thing.

The next day, the husband is at his work.

He finds out about someone whose daughter is having a wedding.

And he talks about ME. "Hey... my wife ships out Gene Ho's stuff all the time. Wow... they do a lot of work. They ship albums all the time."

Now the mom is intrigued. She goes home and Googles my name and finds my website.

Then she tells her daughter: "...Well... everyone is talking about this studio. I just checked out their website. Wow. You should check it out."

See how that works?

I just put three dots between my new client and myself.

Now guess what's going to happen when the mom goes back to the clerk's husband and tells him they just hired me.

He feels like a hero since he "discovered" me.

And now he's more apt to talk about me to others.

The more dots... the more talk.

Granted - I'll take it.

I'll take a wedding going straight from me to my client.

But ideally, I want as many steps between her and I as possible.

I do this when I feel there is an opportunity to do it.

Even when "bad things" come about.

I get all my insurance through one broker.

One company handles my home insurance, business, car, everything.

OK... MOST of my insurance is direct debited from my checking account.

But I still have some that I need to physically write a check to and mail it.

Sometimes I forget to do this.

I'm just very busy.

So one time, one of these insurances lapsed because I didn't pay the bill.

It happens, and it was a big deal.

I'd rather not say which one it was, but basically - you really need to have this insurance.

So I'm freaking out.

And I call up my insurance agent.

And they are fantastic. This is a great company.

So they are in "freak out mode" with me.

And that in itself is a lesson.

Cry with people who cry. Laugh with people who laugh.

But right now? I'm in freak out mode because my insurance just lapsed.

And they went into "freak out mode" with me.

And I appreciated it.

So they are in full alert.

Basically… you don't want a Chinese driver out there without car insurance.

Capiche?

My insurance agent has children out there. This is not a good thing. Warn everyone!

OK…

So everyone is freaking out there.

I'm freaking out.

Finally… they're making phone calls.

And I can't get my insurance reinstated because I've been late a few times paying the bill.

This wasn't the first time I didn't pay on time.

Usually, I get a warning letter in the mail.

I'm sure I got it and ignored it.

Because this time I forgot to pay it.

I'm taking a taxi cab to my studio, OK?

So my old insurance company wouldn't take me back.

And so finally they find a way to get me covered with another company.

Everyone has a big laugh at it at the agency.

I have a big laugh about it.

And truly it's fodder for talk there.

Save Gene Ho! We saved Gene Ho!

So same thing.

I send over Krispy Kreme donuts to their insurance agency and I hand deliver it.

Day over. And it makes for GREAT conversation when they get home to their spouses.

I always look for opportunities to create more dots.

Here's a story from a friend of mine. He's a wedding DJ and a very good one.

His name is Lee Edwards.

He told me a story about how one of the venue coordinators kept recommending him.

The venue was a very prominent wedding location.

And he kept getting jobs there.

Finally, he asked the venue coordinator.

He said… "Why…"

And she interrupted him.

"Why do I keep recommending you?

Wow… read his mind.

She went on to say, "You don't remember me. But way back when, I used to be a bartender for (this other company). Every time you worked with me, you were always nice to me."

See how everything falls into place?

The easy way of doing it is just to be a nice person.

But in general, people aren't stupid.

People realize when you are sucking up to someone because they are important or that they can give you money.

Either be a very nice person in real life - or create your networks based upon people who have nothing to do with you – people with which you have "nothing" to gain.

Both ways work.

Sometimes photographers… especially wedding photographers get a bad rap for being jerks.

Actually, there's a reason for this.

The reason is sometimes we have to be "forceful."

We're there to work, and sometimes to get things done we have to lay the law down.

Some people can take this as being a jerk.

But you have a job to do.

But for the most part? It's easy to be nice when someone is giving you money.

Go beyond that.

Think about creating dots.

Think about creating memorable moments where people will talk about you.

That's what marketing is all about.

Chapter 14

Your Reputation

Ultimately with just about everything you do? It all rests with you.

And you know that.

But what is surprising is how smart the general public is.

They know you more than you realize.

For starters, there's really no two ways around it.

All the marketing in the world won't help if your photography isn't good.

If you're reading this, your work has to be at least halfway decent.

Most photographers don't worry about marketing too much unless they have their basics down.

So I realize you do have to come in with your game face.

You need to be able to shoot.

OK…

So you can.

And that's great.

One thing I realize is how much the general public really knows about you.

And if the public doesn't really know about you – or if there isn't a general consensus about you? Then you just need to shoot more.

So you know what I'm talking about, try this experiment.

Do this in your mind only.

Pick a photographer that you know that is prominent in your area.

Ask yourself... what do you think of this person?

What is his or her reputation?

I bet you come VERY close to the reality.

The reason?

Because you ALSO are the general public.

Your thoughts might run the whole gambit.

It might be anything from:

"This guy is a great photographer, but everyone knows he's a jerk."

"This photographer is the nicest person, but I'm honestly surprised she does well because her photography is weak."

"This photographer has to have the biggest ego in the world, but for sure... he is good. Really good."

Or it can be genuine: "This photographer is the best. And he deserves everything he's got."

The thing is, we all are building a reputation.

It might be good or it might be bad.

Most likely it will be a combination of the two.

I'm actually shocked at how close my reputation matched what was REALLY going on in my career.

But I've always been honest enough to interpret that and make the necessary adjustments in my marketing strategy.

Earlier on in this book, I talked about the time when it took forever to get my albums out.

It was a rotten time in my life.

And I took way too long to get my product out.

The word on the street was that, "Gene Ho is good. But you better be prepared to wait."

At that time? It was pretty darn accurate.

Granted, the bottom line is I really needed to get my product out faster.

So all the marketing in the world wouldn't have made a difference.

I did fix it.

And afterward, I came out with a marketing campaign where I guaranteed return times.

If you want to get the pulse of business… be honest with yourself or simply listen to others.

It's out there. They will tell you. Or you might already know.

But you have a reputation for good, bad or indifferent.

Keep in mind that from time to time, you will get some negative comments about you.

Some of it is legit.

This isn't an easy business to be involved with.

I know you want to please all of your clients.

It's just not possible.

And photographers learn that really quick.

When that happens? The best thing you can do is dig harder.

But as you progress, you're also going to run into jealousy and hate from other photographers.

It's all good. Welcome it.

My viewpoint about them is that as long as they don't run into outright lies - that you should welcome them.

For starters, if you hear of "trash talk" from other photographers… use that as an opportunity.

That is a gold mine for you.

I have ears.

Sometimes people will say that I'm pompous.

I actually WANT people to say that.

Granted. Not my clients. And I hope I'm not.

But I don't mind it when other photographers say that about me.

You want other photographers to talk trash about you.

If that happens to you? Consider it a gift.

This way you can counter that by being the complete opposite.

If they say you're pompous? Make it a point to everyone you meet NOT to be.

But the point being?

It's just some Kung Fu stuff that you're throwing back at everyone.

Basically, you're using their own words against your enemies.

And enemies are really good to have.

Because without them, it's hard to get a feel of what to do.

Not everyone is going to like you.

Actually, you're not going to like everyone.

So don't play into anyone's trap and talk trash.

But hope they talk trash about you.

Because nothing builds word of mouth better than people saying that you're a horrible mess.

Quite frankly, it's the oldest trick in the book.

And that's why you should never fall into the trap.

If you ever get word that "so-and-so" said this or that about you?

Just speak glowingly about "so and so."

You'll make the person who talked trash look like an idiot.

It's a wonderful marketing strategy.

Ultimately, it's all about you and your clients.

Small baby steps. One client at a time.

And as you please them? They will fight for you.

They will tell others about you and your work.

Chapter 15

Photography, Marketing and Me

At the time, I was probably about 28.

I'd already been working as a professional photographer for some time.

I started working professionally at 22.

At the time, I was really starting to make a name for myself in my hometown.

And this was just before the big expansion of my studio.

Back then, I had one studio. Myrtle Beach.

But still, I thought I was a pretty snazzy photographer.

Then I had a conversation with a friend who owned a local photo lab.

"Gene. You are a marketing genius," he said. "That's the difference between you and the other photographers."

Hmm…

At the time it was a unique thought for me.

Up until that time? I thought it was me.

I thought it was my shooting that was making the difference.

Even today... I constantly question myself as a photographer.

I ask myself if I'm special.

Is this something that I'm really gifted at?

I really struggle with that question.

Part of it is my absolute love affair with photography.

I love photography.

And sometimes I wonder if it loves me back with the same passion.

I know that is a strange concept to grasp.

I guess the best way I can articulate what I'm speaking about:

Did you ever hear about an athlete that is just so gifted in a sport?

Like everyone is calling him a natural.

But sometimes that athlete doesn't really respect his own gift.

And he might party. Or maybe he doesn't train right.

Basically... the "sport" loves him more than the athlete loves the sport.

I realize this is a bizarre concept.

But I wonder if I love photography more than photography loves me.

Am I really talented as a photographer? Or did I just love it so much that I tried so amazingly hard at getting good at it.

Some might argue that I have to be gifted in photography.

After all, if I'm a success in it – then certainly I've been blessed with a unique talent.

But I'm not sure.

I really do wonder how much my marketing talent has to do with my success.

Marketing has always been simple for me.

I have no MBA degree.

And as crazy as it seems, I never read marketing books for business in general.

The reason is because I feel I need to go with my instinct.

And I guess that's why I wrote this book this way. Basically sharing principles rather than some step-by-step instructional guide.

I think the best thing I can teach you about marketing - especially when it comes to photography - is that it goes by feel.

At the same time? I think it's something that can be learned.

Maybe learn to develop that instinct.

Make it into a game.

Look around at unrelated businesses.

Look at their marketing strategies.

And ask yourself if you were in charge of their marketing - what would you do differently.

Maybe it's just me.

Maybe it's just me who looks at the world on how "WE" look at businesses and "BUSINESS" look at us.

But I love it.

I love the science behind it.

I'll tell you a story about how this was - WAY before I was ever a photographer.

I was 19 years old.

At the time, I never picked up a camera. I knew nothing about photography.

At the time? I was a Life Guard.

I was a City of Myrtle Beach Life Guard.

And without going through the whys and the hows…

In Myrtle Beach currently - and way back when…

The way the Life Guards get compensated in Myrtle Beach is by renting umbrellas.

So basically you have two jobs.

Your primary job - and it is legit. Your first job is to protect the people in the water in front of you.

I loved that job. And I did it faithfully.

But your second job is to rent umbrellas.

That's the way it is. It's how you earn your money.

Basically, you set up umbrellas in the morning. People rent them. And you get a percentage of what you make.

Way back when, I had Life Guard stand called "First North."

It was named "First North" because it was the stand in front of the road, 1st Ave. North in Myrtle Beach.

OK…

I was given this stand because it was the worst stand for making money.

I was a rookie Life Guard at the time, and all of the veteran Life Guards would pick the big money stands.

So I got stuck with this crappy stand that made no money.

But as soon as I took over the stand - I turned it into a moneymaker.

At the time, the stand was notorious for not making money. But I made it work.

OK… this will be a fun game for us.

From what you learned… can you think what I did to make a difference?

I'm sure you could think of a few things.

But I will tell you what I did - and you can see my marketing skills in action.

This is how I increased the number of people renting umbrellas and thus - increasing my percentage as well as my tips.

I had an idea.

I saw all the people sitting on the beach. And I saw opportunity.

The first morning I took over the stand… I set up what we called 6 and 6.

That is 6 umbrellas to the left of my Life Guard stand and 6 to the right of it.

Three or four people rented the umbrella (that also came with two chairs.)

OK… so even as a young 19-year-old Life Guard. Me. Gene Ho. Life Guard extraordinaire.

I had an idea.

How could I get all these other people sitting on the beach to rent my umbrellas?

Well, it's certainly not because they wanted to stay out of the sun.

Everyone was there to enjoy the water and get a tan.

So I had an idea.

In the middle of the day, I would do a "round."

I bought these plastic cups. And I filled up a big red container filled with ice water.

And each day, at 11 a.m. and at 3 p.m., I would make my rounds.

I would stop what I was doing, and make a big show of putting up my "off duty" sign.

Because back then, Gene Ho was a strapping young morsel of man meat, I would walk past all the other beach goers who didn't rent my umbrellas.

And I would walk past them with my plastic cups and my red container.

And I'd talk to each one of my renters.

"Hello sir. Would you like some ice water?"

And one by one? I would do my routine.

After day two?

Everyone that went out there every day would see my routine.

Twice a day. Once at 11 a.m. and once at 3 p.m.

Huh…

Wow. Wow, right?

Sure. Think about what everyone ELSE was thinking on that beach?

Wow. You rent an umbrella? And suddenly you're like some VIP.

And I would love it when I would finish my rounds. And feign walking back to my stand - only to hear one of my renters have to say twice… "Life Guard. More water please!"

Ah… love it.

Say it louder please, sir?

Let everyone here in my section of the beach know that you rent an umbrella from me? You will indeed be treated like royalty.

So maybe I've always had it in me.

But it was then I learned the difference between marketing and advertising.

Back then? There were other Life Guards. And I remember they would put on their chairs - "Tips Appreciated."

I never needed to do that.

I got them anyway.

And I rented new umbrellas week by week.

If I started my Monday with 6 at 6? By week's end - I stretched it to 15 and 15.

That's what it's all about.

Are we learning to be some charlatan?

No way.

I don't teach people how to swindle people.

Here's the difference.

Imagine TWO identical products.

If you want to?

Two umbrellas on the beach.

One is at the far SOUTH end of my umbrella line that I control.

The other is on the far NORTH end of the umbrella line that my fellow lifeguard controls.

Two identical products.

My question is why would you choose MY umbrella over the next Life Guard's umbrella? It's because of the way I present my product.

And THAT is why marketing makes all the difference in the world.

In photography, there are great differences in both styles and service.

There is a great difference in product.

And to be honest, sometimes it overlaps.

I use the analogy of a flower.

Take a flower. And take the any five photographers that you know - that you think are about at the same skill level as you.

So you have a flower and five photographers.

Each gets 10 shots at it.

Be honest with yourself…

If each gets 10 submissions… how different do you think they would be?

What I suspect?

I suspect that there would be very little between all of them.

Granted… I get it.

We're not shooting flowers.

We're shooting people. We're shooting weddings.

My point being… Yes.

I understand that this is still about our work.

It's still about our photography.

But given two different products - that is, one that you did. And one that your competition did…

Say it's close. Real close.

What will make the difference?

Marketing. Or how one picture is presented over another.

It's the same as why someone would rent YOUR umbrella seat over one that's five feet away.

And sure…

There are other factors that go into it.

Customer service. Rapport.

But marketing gives you the edge.

And I really believe it has given me the edge over the years.

That being said?

I want to thank you from the bottom of my heart for reading this book.

As you know, this is a labor of love for me.

So thank you. Happy shooting.

And make your clients love you.

www.ingramcontent.com/pod-product-compliance
Lightning Source LLC
Chambersburg PA
CBHW021941170526
45157CB00003B/880